The Works of
Alice Dunbar-Nelson

THE SCHOMBURG LIBRARY OF
NINETEENTH-CENTURY BLACK WOMEN WRITERS

General Editor, Henry Louis Gates, Jr.

Titles are listed chronologically; collections that include works published over a span of years are listed according to the publication date of their initial work.

The Works

of

Alice Dunbar-Nelson

Volume 1

Edited by
GLORIA T. HULL

❧ ❧ ❧

❧ ❧ ❧

New York   Oxford
OXFORD UNIVERSITY PRESS
1988

Oxford University Press

Oxford   New York   Toronto
Delhi   Bombay   Calcutta   Madras   Karachi
Petaling Jaya   Singapore   Hong Kong   Tokyo
Nairobi   Dar es Salaam   Cape Town
Melbourne   Auckland

and associated companies in
Beirut   Berlin   Ibadan   Nicosia

Published by Oxford University Press, Inc.,
200 Madison Avenue, New York, New York 10016

Oxford is a registered trademark of Oxford University Press

Library of Congress Cataloging-in-Publication Data

Dunbar-Nelson, Alice Moore, 1875–1935.
The works of Alice Dunbar-Nelson.
(The Schomburg library on nineteenth-century black
women writers)
1. Afro-Americans—Literary collections.   I. Hull,
Gloria T.   II. Title.   III. Series.
PS3507.U6228   1988   818'.5209   87-14118
ISBN 0-19-505250-1 (v. 1)
ISBN 0-19-505267-6 (set)

2 4 6 8 10 9 7 5 3 1

Printed in the United States of America
on acid-free paper

The
Schomburg Library
of
Nineteenth-Century
Black Women Writers
is
Dedicated
in Memory
of
PAULINE AUGUSTA COLEMAN GATES

1916–1987

PUBLISHER'S NOTE

FOREWORD
In Her Own Write

Henry Louis Gates, Jr.

One muffled strain in the Silent South, a jarring chord and a vague and uncomprehended cadenza has been and still is the Negro. And of that muffled chord, the one mute and voiceless note has been the sadly expectant Black Woman, ...

The "other side" has not been represented by one who "lives there." And not many can more sensibly realize and more accurately tell the weight and the fret of the "long dull pain" than the open-eyed but hitherto voiceless Black Woman of America.

. . . as our Caucasian barristers are not to blame if they cannot *quite* put themselves in the dark man's place, neither should the dark man be wholly expected fully and adequately to reproduce the exact Voice of the Black Woman.

—ANNA JULIA COOPER, *A Voice From the South* (1892)

The birth of the Afro-American literary tradition occurred in 1773, when Phillis Wheatley published a book of poetry. Despite the fact that her book garnered for her a remarkable amount of attention, Wheatley's journey to the printer had been a most arduous one. Sometime in 1772, a young African girl walked demurely into a room in Boston to undergo an oral examination, the results of which would determine the direction of her life and work. Perhaps she was shocked upon entering the appointed room. For there, perhaps gathered in a semicircle, sat eighteen of Boston's most notable citizens. Among them were John Erving, a prominent Boston merchant; the Reverend Charles Chauncy, pastor of the Tenth Congregational Church; and John Hancock, who would later gain fame for his signature on the Declaration of Independence. At the center of this group was His Excellency, Thomas Hutchinson, governor of Massachusetts, with Andrew Oliver, his lieutenant governor, close by his side.

Why had this august group been assembled? Why had it seen fit to summon this young African girl, scarcely eighteen years old, before it? This group of "the most respectable Characters in *Boston*," as it would later define itself, had assembled to question closely the African adolescent on the slender sheaf of poems that she claimed to have "written by herself." We can only speculate on the nature of the questions posed to the fledgling poet. Perhaps they asked her to identify and explain—for all to hear—exactly who were the Greek and Latin gods and poets alluded to so frequently in her work. Perhaps they asked her to conjugate a verb in Latin or even to translate randomly selected passages from the Latin, which she and her master, John Wheatley, claimed that she "had made some Progress in." Or perhaps they asked her to recite from memory key passages from the texts of John Milton and Alexander Pope, the two poets by whom the African claimed to be most directly influenced. We do not know.

We do know, however, that the African poet's responses were more than sufficient to prompt the eighteen august gentlemen to compose, sign, and publish a two-paragraph "Attestation," an open letter "To the Publick" that prefaces Phillis Wheatley's book and that reads in part:

> We whose Names are under-written, do assure the World, that the Poems specified in the following Page, were (as we

verily believe) written by Phillis, a young Negro Girl, who
was but a few Years since, brought an uncultivated Barbarian
from *Africa*, and has ever since been, and now is, under the
Disadvantage of serving as a Slave in a Family in this Town.
She has been examined by some of the best Judges, and is
thought qualified to write them.

So important was this document in securing a publisher for
Wheatley's poems that it forms the signal element in the
prefatory matter preceding her *Poems on Various Subjects, Religious and Moral*, published in London in 1773.

Without the published "Attestation," Wheatley's publisher
claimed, few would believe that an African could possibly
have written poetry all by herself. As the eighteen put the
matter clearly in their letter, "Numbers would be ready to
suspect they were not really the Writings of Phillis." Wheatley and her master, John Wheatley, had attempted to publish
a similar volume in 1772 in Boston, but Boston publishers
had been incredulous. One year later, "Attestation" in hand,
Phillis Wheatley and her master's son, Nathaniel Wheatley,
sailed for England, where they completed arrangements for
the publication of a volume of her poems with the aid of the
Countess of Huntington and the Earl of Dartmouth.

This curious anecdote, surely one of the oddest oral ex-
aminations on record, is only a tiny part of a larger, and
even more curious, episode in the Enlightenment. Since the
beginning of the sixteenth century, Europeans had wondered aloud whether or not the African "species of men," as
they were most commonly called, *could* ever create formal
literature, could ever master "the arts and sciences." If they
could, the argument ran, then the African variety of humanity was fundamentally related to the European variety. If not,
then it seemed clear that the African was destined by nature

to be a slave. This was the burden shouldered by Phillis Wheatley when she successfully defended herself and the authorship of her book against counterclaims and doubts.

Indeed, with her successful defense, Wheatley launched two traditions at once—the black American literary tradition *and* the black woman's literary tradition. If it is extraordinary that not just one but both of these traditions were founded simultaneously by a black woman—certainly an event unique in the history of literature—it is also ironic that this important fact of common, coterminous literary origins seems to have escaped most scholars.

That the progenitor of the black literary tradition was a woman means, in the most strictly literal sense, that all subsequent black writers have evolved in a matrilinear line of descent, and that each, consciously or unconsciously, has extended and revised a canon whose foundation was the poetry of a black woman. Early black writers seem to have been keenly aware of Wheatley's founding role, even if most of her white reviewers were more concerned with the implications of her race than her gender. Jupiter Hammon, for example, whose 1760 broadside "An Evening Thought. Salvation by Christ, With Penitential Cries" was the first individual poem published by a black American, acknowledged Wheatley's influence by selecting her as the subject of his second broadside, "An Address to Miss Phillis Wheatly [*sic*], Ethiopian Poetess, in Boston," which was published at Hartford in 1778. And George Moses Horton, the second Afro-American to publish a book of poetry in English (1829), brought out in 1838 an edition of his *Poems By A Slave* bound together with Wheatley's work. Indeed, for fifty-six years, between 1773 and 1829, when Horton published *The Hope of Liberty*, Wheatley was the *only* black person to have published a book of imaginative literature in English. So central was this black woman's role in the shaping of the Afro-American literary tradition that, as one historian has maintained, the history of the reception of Phillis Wheatley's poetry *is* the history of Afro-American literary criticism. Well into the nineteenth century, Wheatley and the black literary tradition were the same entity.

But Wheatley is not the only black woman writer who stands as a pioneering figure in Afro-American literature. Just as Wheatley gave birth to the genre of black poetry, Ann Plato was the first Afro-American to publish a book of essays (1841) and Harriet E. Wilson was the first black person to publish a novel in the United States (1859).

Despite this pioneering role of black women in the tradition, however, many of their contributions before this century have been all but lost or unrecognized. As Hortense Spillers observed as recently as 1983,

> With the exception of a handful of autobiographical narratives from the nineteenth century, the black woman's realities are virtually suppressed until the period of the Harlem Renaissance and later. Essentially the black woman as artist, as intellectual spokesperson for her own cultural apprenticeship, has not existed before, for anyone. At the source of [their] own symbol-making task, [the community of black women writers] confronts, therefore, a tradition of work that is quite recent, its continuities, broken and sporadic.

Until now, it has been extraordinarily difficult to establish the formal connections between early black women's writing and that of the present, precisely because our knowledge of their work has been broken and sporadic. Phillis Wheatley, for example, while certainly the most reprinted and discussed poet in the tradition, is also one of the least understood. Ann Plato's seminal work, *Essays* (which includes biographies and poems), has not been reprinted since it was published a cen-

tury and a half ago. And Harriet Wilson's *Our Nig,* her
compelling novel of a black woman's expanding consciousness in a racist Northern antebellum environment, never received even *one* review or comment at a time when virtually
all works written by black people were heralded by abolition-
ists as salient arguments against the existence of human slavery. Many of the books reprinted in this set experienced a
similar fate, the most dreadful fate for an author: that of
being ignored then relegated to the obscurity of the rare book
section of a university library. We can only wonder how
many other texts in the black woman's tradition have been
lost to this generation of readers or remain unclassified or
uncatalogued and, hence, unread.

This was not always so, however. Black women writers
dominated the final decade of the nineteenth century, perhaps
spurred to publish by an 1886 essay entitled "The Coming
American Novelist," which was published in *Lippincott's
Monthly Magazine* and written by "A Lady From Philadelphia." This pseudonymous essay argued that the "Great
American Novel" would be written by a black person. Her
argument is so curious that it deserves to be repeated:

> When we come to formulate our demands of the Coming
> American Novelist, we will agree that he must be native-
> born. His ancestors may come from where they will, but we
> must give him a birthplace and have the raising of him. Still,
> the longer his family has been here the better he will represent
> us. Suppose he should have no country but ours, no traditions
> but those he has learned here, no longings apart from us, no
> future except in our future—the orphan of the world, he
> finds with us his home. And with all this, suppose he refuses
> to be fused into that grand conglomerate we call the "Amer-
> ican type." With us, he is not of us. He is original, he has
> humor, he is tender, he is passive and fiery, he has been

taught what we call justice, and he has his own opinion about it. He has suffered everything a poet, a dramatist, a novelist need suffer before he comes to have his lips anointed. And with it all he is in one sense a spectator, a little out of the race. How would these conditions go towards forming an original development? In a word, suppose the coming novelist is of African origin? When one comes to consider the subject, there is no improbability in it. One thing is certain,—our great novel will not be written by the typical American.

An atypical American, indeed. Not only would the great American novel be written by an African-American, it would be written by an African-American *woman:*

Yet farther: I have used the generic masculine pronoun because it is convenient; but Fate keeps revenge in store. It was a woman who, taking the wrongs of the African as her theme, wrote the novel that awakened the world to their reality, and why should not the coming novelist be a woman as well as an African? She—the woman of that race—has some claims on Fate which are not yet paid up.

It is these claims on fate that we seek to pay by publishing The Schomburg Library of Nineteenth-Century Black Women Writers.

This theme would be repeated by several black women authors, most notably by Anna Julia Cooper, a prototypical black feminist whose 1892 *A Voice From the South* can be considered to be one of the original texts of the black feminist movement. It was Cooper who first analyzed the fallacy of referring to "the Black man" when speaking of black people and who argued that just as white men cannot speak through the consciousness of black men, neither can black *men* "fully and adequately . . . reproduce the exact Voice of the Black Woman." Gender and race, she argues, cannot be conflated, except in the instance of a black woman's voice, and it is this voice which must be uttered and to which we must listen. As Cooper puts the matter so compellingly:

> It is not the intelligent woman vs. the ignorant woman; nor the white woman vs. the black, the brown, and the red,—it is not even the cause of woman vs. man. Nay, 'tis woman's strongest vindication for speaking that *the world needs to hear her voice*. It would be subversive of every human interest that the cry of one-half the human family be stifled. Woman in stepping from the pedestal of statue-like inactivity in the domestic shrine, and daring to think and move and speak,— to undertake to help shape, mold, and direct the thought of her age, is merely completing the circle of the world's vision. Hers is every interest that has lacked an interpreter and a defender. Her cause is linked with that of every agony that has been dumb—every wrong that needs a voice.
>
> It is no fault of man's that he has not been able to see truth from her standpoint. It does credit both to his head and heart that no greater mistakes have been committed or even wrongs perpetrated while she sat making tatting and snipping paper flowers. Man's own innate chivalry and the mutual interdependence of their interests have insured his treating her cause, in the main at least, as his own. And he is pardonably surprised and even a little chagrined, perhaps, to find his legislation not considered "perfectly lovely" in every respect. But in any case his work is only impoverished by her remaining dumb. The world has had to limp along with the wobbling gait and one-sided hesitancy of a man with one eye. Suddenly the bandage is removed from the other eye and the whole body is filled with light. It sees a circle where before it saw a segment. The darkened eye restored, every member rejoices with it.

The myopic sight of the darkened eye can only be restored when the full range of the black woman's voice, with its own special timbres and shadings, remains mute no longer.

Similarly, Victoria Earle Matthews, an author of short stories and essays, and a cofounder in 1896 of the National Association of Colored Women, wrote in her stunning essay, "The Value of Race Literature" (1895), that "when the literature of our race is developed, it will of necessity be different in all essential points of greatness, true heroism and real Christianity from what we may at the present time, for convenience, call American literature." Matthews argued that this great tradition of Afro-American literature would be the textual outlet "for the unnaturally suppressed inner lives which our people have been compelled to lead." Once these "unnaturally suppressed inner lives" of black people are unveiled, no "grander diffusion of mental light" will shine more brightly, she concludes, than that of the articulate Afro-American woman:

And now comes the question, What part shall we women play in the Race Literature of the future? . . . within the compass of one small journal ["Woman's Era"] we have struck out a new line of departure—a journal, a record of Race interests gathered from all parts of the United States, carefully selected, moistened, winnowed and garnered by the ablest intellects of educated colored women, shrinking at no lofty theme, shirking no serious duty, aiming at every possible excellence, and determined to do their part in the future uplifting of the race.

If twenty women, by their concentrated efforts in one literary movement, can meet with such success as has engendered, planned out, and so successfully consummated this convention, what much more glorious results, what wider spread success, what grander diffusion of mental light will not come forth at the bidding of the enlarged hosts of women writers, already called into being by the stimulus of your efforts?

And here let me speak one word for my journalistic sisters

who have already entered the broad arena of journalism.
Before the "Woman's Era" had come into existence, no one
except themselves can appreciate the bitter experience and
sore disappointments under which they have at all times been
compelled to pursue their chosen vocations.

If their brothers of the press have had their difficulties to
contend with, I am here as a sister journalist to state, from
the fullness of knowledge, that their task has been an easy
one compared with that of the colored woman in journalism.

Woman's part in Race Literature, as in Race building, is
the most important part and has been so in all ages. . . . All
through the most remote epochs she has done her share in
literature. . . .

One of the most important aspects of this set is the repub-
lication of the salient texts from 1890 to 1910, which literary
historians could well call "The Black Woman's Era." In addition to Mary Helen Washington's definitive edition of
Cooper's *A Voice From the South*, we have reprinted two novels by Amelia Johnson, Frances Harper's *Iola Leroy*, two
novels by Emma Dunham Kelley, Alice Dunbar-Nelson's two
impressive collections of short stories, and Pauline Hopkins's
three serialized novels as well as her monumental novel,
Contending Forces—all published between 1890 and 1910. Indeed, black women published more works of fiction in these
two decades than black men had published in the previous
half century. Nevertheless, this great achievement has been
ignored.

Moreover, the writings of nineteenth-century Afro-
American women in general have remained buried in obscurity, accessible only in research libraries or in overpriced and
poorly edited reprints. Many of these books have never been
reprinted at all; in some instances only one or two copies are
extant. In these works of fiction, poetry, autobiography, bi-

ography, essays, and journalism resides the mind of the nineteenth-century Afro-American woman. Until these works are made readily available to teachers and their students, a significant segment of the black tradition will remain silent.

Oxford University Press, in collaboration with the Schomburg Center for Research in Black Culture, is publishing thirty volumes of these compelling works, each of which contains an introduction by an expert in the field. The set includes such rare texts as Johnson's *The Hazeley Family* and *Clarence and Corinne,* Plato's *Essays,* the most complete edition of Phillis Wheatley's poems and letters, Emma Dunham Kelley's pioneering novel *Megda,* several previously unpublished stories and a novel by Alice Dunbar-Nelson, and the first collected volumes of Pauline Hopkins's three serialized novels and Frances Harper's poetry. We also present four volumes of poetry by such women as Mary Eliza Tucker Lambert, Adah Menken, Josephine Heard, and Maggie Johnson. Numerous slave and spiritual narratives, a newly discovered novel—*Four Girls at Cottage City*—by Emma Dunham Kelley (-Hawkins), and the first American edition of *Wonderful Adventures of Mrs. Seacole in Many Lands* are also among the texts included.

In addition to resurrecting the works of black women authors, it is our hope that this set will facilitate the resurrection of the Afro-American woman's literary tradition itself by unearthing its nineteenth-century roots. In the works of Nella Larsen and Jessie Fauset, Zora Neale Hurston and Ann Petry, Lorraine Hansberry and Gwendolyn Brooks, Paule Marshall and Toni Cade Bambara, Audre Lorde and Rita Dove, Toni Morrison and Alice Walker, Gloria Naylor and Jamaica Kincaid, these roots have branched luxuriantly. The eighteenth- and nineteenth-century authors whose works are presented in this set founded and nurtured the black women's literary tradition, which must be revived, explicated, analyzed, and debated before we can understand more completely the formal shaping of this tradition within a tradition, a coded literary universe through which, regrettably, we are only just beginning to navigate our way. As Anna Cooper said nearly one hundred years ago, we have been blinded by the loss of sight in one eye and have therefore been unable to detect the full *shape* of the Afro-American literary tradition.

Literary works configure into a tradition not because of some mystical collective unconscious determined by the biology of race or gender, but because writers read other writers and *ground* their representations of experience in models of language provided largely by other writers to whom they feel akin. It is through this mode of literary revision, amply evident in the *texts* themselves—in formal echoes, recast metaphors, even in parody—that a "tradition" emerges and defines itself.

This is formal bonding, and it is only through formal bonding that we can know a literary tradition. The collective publication of these works by black women now, for the first time, makes it possible for scholars and critics, male and female, black and white, to *demonstrate* that black women writers read, and revised, other black women writers. To demonstrate this set of formal literary relations is to demonstrate that sexuality, race, and gender are both the condition and the basis of *tradition*—but tradition as found in discrete acts of language use.

A word is in order about the history of this set. For the past decade, I have taught a course, first at Yale and then at Cornell, entitled "Black Women and Their Fictions," a course that I inherited from Toni Morrison, who developed it in the mid-1970s for Yale's Program in Afro-American Studies. Although the course was inspired by the remarkable accomplishments of black women novelists since 1970, I gradually extended its beginning date to the late nineteenth century, studying Frances Harper's *Iola Leroy* and Anna Julia Cooper's *A Voice From the South*, both published in 1892. With the discovery of Harriet E. Wilson's seminal novel, *Our Nig* (1859), and Jean Yellin's authentication of Harriet Jacobs's brilliant slave narrative, *Incidents in the Life of a Slave Girl* (1861), a survey course spanning over a century and a quarter emerged.

But the discovery of *Our Nig,* as well as the interest in nineteenth-century black women's writing that this discovery generated, convinced me that even the most curious and diligent scholars knew very little of the extensive history of the creative writings of Afro-American women before 1900. Indeed, most scholars of Afro-American literature had never even read most of the books published by black women, simply because these books—of poetry, novels, short stories, essays, and autobiography—were mostly accessible only in rare book sections of university libraries. For reasons unclear to me even today, few of these marvelous renderings of the Afro-American woman's consciousness were reprinted in the late 1960s and early 1970s, when so many other texts of the Afro-American literary tradition were resurrected from the dark and silent graveyard of the out-of-print and were reissued in facsimile editions aimed at the hungry readership for canonical texts in the nascent field of black studies.

So, with the help of several superb research assistants—including David Curtis, Nicola Shilliam, Wendy Jones, Sam Otter, Janadas Devan, Suvir Kaul, Cynthia Bond, Elizabeth Alexander, and Adele Alexander—and with the expert advice of scholars such as William Robinson, William Andrews, Mary Helen Washington, Maryemma Graham, Jean Yellin, Houston A. Baker, Jr., Richard Yarborough, Hazel Carby, Joan R. Sherman, Frances Foster, and William French, dozens of bibliographies were used to compile a list of books written or narrated by black women mostly before 1910. Without the assistance provided through this shared experience of scholarship, the scholar's true legacy, this project could not have been conceived. As the list grew, I was struck by how very many of these titles that I, for example, had never even heard of, let alone read, such as Ann Plato's *Essays*, Louisa Picquet's slave narrative, or Amelia Johnson's two novels, *Clarence and Corinne* and *The Hazeley Family*. Through our research with the Black Periodical Fiction and Poetry Project (funded by NEH and the Ford Foundation), I also realized that several novels by black women, including three works of fiction by Pauline Hopkins, had been serialized in black periodicals, but had never been collected and published as books. Nor had the several books of poetry published by black women, such as the prolific Frances E. W. Harper, been collected and edited. When I discovered still another "lost" novel by an Afro-American woman (*Four Girls at Cottage City*, published in 1898 by Emma Dunham Kelley-Hawkins), I decided to attempt to edit a collection of reprints of these works and to publish them as a "library" of black women's writings, in part so that I could read them myself.

Convincing university and trade publishers to undertake this project proved to be a difficult task. Despite the commercial success of *Our Nig* and of the several reprint series of women's works (such as Virago, the Beacon Black Women Writers Series, and Rutgers' American Women Writers Series), several presses rejected the project as "too large," "too limited," or as "commercially unviable." Only two publishers recognized the viability and the import of the project and, of these, Oxford's commitment to publish the titles simultaneously as a set made the press's offer irresistible.

While attempting to locate original copies of these exceedingly rare books, I discovered that most of the texts were housed at the Schomburg Center for Research in Black Culture, a branch of The New York Public Library, under the direction of Howard Dodson. Dodson's infectious enthusiasm for the project and his generous collaboration, as well as that of his stellar staff (especially Diana Lachatanere, Sharon Howard, Ellis Haizip, Richard Newman, and Betty Gubert), led to a joint publishing initiative that produced this set as part of the Schomburg's major fund-raising campaign. Without Dodson's foresight and generosity of spirit, the set would not have materialized. Without William P. Sisler's masterful editorship at Oxford and his staff's careful attention to detail, the set would have remained just another grand idea that tends to languish in a scholar's file cabinet.

I would also like to thank Dr. Michael Winston and Dr. Thomas C. Battle, Vice-President of Academic Affairs and the Director of the Moorland-Spingarn Research Center (respectively) at Howard University, for their unending encouragement, support, and collaboration in this project, and Esme E. Bhan at Howard for her meticulous research and bibliographical skills. In addition, I would like to acknowledge the aid of the staff at the libraries of Duke University, Cornell University (especially Tom Weissinger and Donald Eddy), the Boston Public Library, the Western Reserve Historical Society, the Library of Congress, and Yale University. Linda Robbins, Marion Osmun, Sarah Flanagan, and Gerard Case, all members of the staff at Oxford, were

extraordinarily effective at coordinating, editing, and producing the various segments of each text in the set. Candy
Ruck, Nina de Tar, and Phillis Molock expertly typed reams
of correspondence and manuscripts connected to the project.

I would also like to express my gratitude to my colleagues
who edited and introduced the individual titles in the set.
Without their attention to detail, their willingness to meet
strict deadlines, and their sheer enthusiasm for this project,
the set could not have been published. But finally and ultimately, I would hope that the publication of the set would
help to generate even more scholarly interest in the black
women authors whose work is presented here. Struggling
against the seemingly insurmountable barriers of racism *and*
sexism, while often raising families and fulfilling full-time
professional obligations, these women managed nevertheless
to record their thoughts and feelings and to *testify* to all who
dare read them that the will to harness the power of collective
endurance and survival is the will to write.

The Schomburg Library of Nineteenth-Century Black
Women Writers is dedicated in memory of Pauline Augusta
Coleman Gates, who died in the spring of 1987. It was she
who inspired in me the love of learning and the love of literature. I have encountered in the books of this set no will
more determined, no courage more noble, no mind more
sublime, no self more celebratory of the achievements of all
Afro-American women, and indeed of life itself, than her
own.

A NOTE FROM
THE SCHOMBURG CENTER

Howard Dodson

The Schomburg Center for Research in Black Culture, The New York Public Library, is pleased to join with Dr. Henry Louis Gates and Oxford University Press in presenting The Schomburg Library of Nineteenth-Century Black Women Writers. This thirty-volume set includes the work of a generation of black women whose writing has only been available previously in rare book collections. The materials reprinted in twenty-four of the thirty volumes are drawn from the unique holdings of the Schomburg Center.

A research unit of The New York Public Library, the Schomburg Center has been in the forefront of those institutions dedicated to collecting, preserving, and providing access to the records of the black past. In the course of its two generations of acquisition and conservation activity, the Center has amassed collections totaling more than 5 million items. They include over 100,000 bound volumes, 85,000 reels and sets of microforms, 300 manuscript collections containing some 3.5 million items, 300,000 photographs and extensive holdings of prints, sound recordings, film and videotape, newspapers, artworks, artifacts, and other book and nonbook materials. Together they vividly document the history and cultural heritages of people of African descent worldwide.

Though established some sixty-two years ago, the Center's book collections date from the sixteenth century. Its oldest item, an Ethiopian Coptic Tunic, dates from the eighth or ninth century. Rare materials, however, are most available for the nineteenth-century African-American experience. It is from these holdings that the majority of the titles selected for inclusion in this set are drawn.

The nineteenth century was a formative period in African-American literary and cultural history. Prior to the Civil War, the majority of black Americans living in the United States were held in bondage. Law and practice forbade teaching them to read or write. Even after the war, many of the impediments to learning and literary productivity remained. Nevertheless, black men and women of the nineteenth century persevered in both areas. Moreover, more African-Americans than we yet realize turned their observations, feelings, social viewpoints, and creative impulses into published works. In time, this nineteenth-century printed record included poetry, short stories, histories, novels, autobiographies, social criticism, and theology, as well as economic and philosophical treatises. Unfortunately, much of this body of literature remained, until very recently, relatively inaccessible to twentieth-century scholars, teachers, creative artists, and others interested in black life. Prior to the late 1960s, most Americans (black as well as white) had never heard of these nineteenth-century authors, much less read their works.

The civil rights and black power movements created unprecedented interest in the thought, behavior, and achievements of black people. Publishers responded by revising traditional texts, introducing the American public to a new generation of African-American writers, publishing a variety of thematic anthologies, and reprinting a plethora of "classic texts" in African-American history, literature, and art. The reprints usually appeared as individual titles or in a series of bound volumes or microform formats.

The Schomburg Center, which has a long history of supporting publishing that deals with the history and culture of Africans in diaspora, became an active participant in many of the reprint revivals of the 1960s. Since hard copies of original printed works are the preferred formats for producing facsimile reproductions, publishers frequently turned to the Schomburg Center for copies of these original titles. In addition to providing such material, Schomburg Center staff members offered advice and consultation, wrote introductions, and occasionally entered into formal copublishing arrangements in some projects.

Most of the nineteenth-century titles reprinted during the 1960s, however, were by and about black men. A few black women were included in the longer series, but works by lesser known black women were generally overlooked. The Schomburg Library of Nineteenth-Century Black Women Writers is both a corrective to these previous omissions and an important contribution to Afro-American literary history in its own right. Through this collection of volumes, the thoughts, perspectives, and creative abilities of nineteenth-century African-American women, as captured in books and pamphlets published in large part before 1910, are again being made available to the general public. The Schomburg Center is pleased to be a part of this historic endeavor.

I would like to thank Professor Gates for initiating this project. Thanks are due both to him and Mr. William P. Sisler of Oxford University Press for giving the Schomburg Center an opportunity to play such a prominent role in the set. Thanks are also due to my colleagues at The New York Public Library and the Schomburg Center, especially Dr. Vartan Gregorian, Richard De Gennaro, Paul Fasana, Betsy

Pinover, Richard Newman, Diana Lachatanere, Glenderlyn Johnson, and Harold Anderson for their assistance and support. I can think of no better way of demonstrating than in this set the role the Schomburg Center plays in assuring that the black heritage will be available for future generations.

CONTENTS

INTRODUCTION

Gloria T. Hull

One senses in practically everything that Alice Dunbar-Nelson wrote a driving desire to pull together the multiple strands of her complex personality and poetics. Yet this desire seems to be undercut or subverted by an opposing—and perhaps ultimately more powerful—ambivalence (I want to say schizophrenia) that makes W. E. B. Du Bois's racially "warring bloods" and Virginia Woolf's female "contrary instincts" look simple. Dunbar-Nelson spent her life assiduously writing herself both into and out of her literary "fictions," using conventional concepts of form, genre, and propriety that (given her lack of creative genius) bound her to divisiveness and inarticulation. This scenario becomes all the more complicated when one remembers that it was played in a late-nineteenth-, early-twentieth-century world where social conditions and the literary establishment made authentic self-definition (as persons and artists) extremely difficult for black women writers.

Dunbar-Nelson began her life as Alice Ruth Moore on July 19, 1875, in New Orleans, Louisiana—marked from the beginning by the mixed white, black, and Indian of her Creole ancestral strains.[1] This mixture endowed her with reddish-blonde baby curls and a fair enough complexion to pass occasionally for white when she was an adult intent on imbibing the high culture (operas, bathing spas, art museums) of the Jim Crow United States society, which was just as committed to her exclusion. Evidence suggests that—a feeling of shame about some circumstance(s) of her birth notwithstanding—she preferred her mixed racial appearance and sometimes looked down on darker skinned blacks, especially if they were also less educated and refined. (Skin color and status were often connected in those early postbellum times. Many progressive colored people believed that the best way to prove their worth was to be as little black as possible, black being equated with narrowness and limitation.) Nevertheless, Dunbar-Nelson fought for the rights of black people in a variety of individual and organizational ways ranging from the women's club movement, to the Dyer Anti-Lynching Bill, to financially aiding, from her own shallow pocket, young charges at the Industrial School for Colored Girls, which she helped to found. She was generally active on behalf of women, motivated by genuine feminist instincts and the available avenues for sociopolitical work. Making a living also occupied and preoccupied her. She was a teacher, stenographer, executive secretary, editor, newspaper columnist, platform speaker, and campaign manager.

All of this reminds us that Dunbar-Nelson perforce wrote in the interstices of a busy existence unsupported (except for one brief period) by any of the money or leisure traditionally associated with people of letters. Doggedly determined to be an author, she plied her trade, often too facilely, hastily, opportunistically, and without revision—carried forward on the flow of words that came quite easily for her. Interestingly enough, she called all of her writing "producing literature," in a humorously ironic leveling of forms and types. But just as ironically, her status is lowered since the more belletristic genres of poetry and fiction are more valued than the noncanonical forms—notably the diary and journalistic essay—that claimed so much of her attention.

Dunbar-Nelson began her career early. As a daring young

author "just on the threshold of life," she published *Violets and Other Tales** in 1895 when she was barely twenty years old. A potpourri of short stories, sketches, essays, reviews, and poetry, this volume is interesting and promising juvenilia wherein the budding writer tries out many voices. Even this early, some of her lifelong characteristics are evident: wide reading and love of books ("Salammbo"); catholicity of intellect ("Unknown Life of Jesus Christ," "Anarchy Alley," "Ten Minutes' Musing"); alienation from her own autobiography and mundane experience; Creole materials and themes ("Titee," "A Carnival Jangle," "Little Miss Sophie"); competence in many genres; use of standard lyric themes; a leaning toward the romantic; ambivalence about woman's concept of self and proper role in the emerging modern world ("Violets," "The Woman," "At Eventide," etc.); a felicitous prose style; and a tendency to pay obeisance to literary and social proprieties. Summarizing the work in this way suggests that it is most profitably read as a precursor of later work, or consulted in retrospect for its revelations of Dunbar-Nelson's roots.

Dunbar-Nelson's second book, *The Goodness of St. Rocque and Other Stories* (Vol. 1, WADN), appeared four years later. Thus, the only two volumes of her own work published during her lifetime (which have kept her writings marginally accessible to later generations of scholars and readers) were printed at the very beginning of her career—before the turn of the century and before books by black writers ceased to be novelties during the "New Negro" era. Therefore, Dunbar-Nelson, in her way, helped to create a black short-story

---

* Included in Volume 1, *The Works of Alice Dunbar-Nelson*, hereafter cited as WADN.

tradition for a reading public conditioned to expect only plantation and minstrel stereotypes. Her strategy for escaping these odious expectations was to eschew black characters and culture and to write, instead, charming, aracial, Creole sketches that solidified her in the then-popular, "female-suitable" local color mode. In the words of one contemporary reviewer, these are

> delightful Creole stories, all bright and full of the true Creole air of easy-going . . . brief and pleasing, instinct with the passion and romance of the people who will ever be associated with such names as Bayou Teche and Lake Pontchartrain.[2]

In part, this sprightly description of the book is accurate. One thinks, for example, of "Titee" (a story that was printed first in *Violets* and then here, with a revised, happy ending). The colorful young hero with a tender heart is eventually rewarded for his self-sacrificing faithfulness to an old derelict as he roams the bayous and canals. Further, the surfaces of all the stories so coruscate with South Louisiana flavor that they give an impression of superficial charm and pleasantness. Yet the truth of the matter is that this apparent brightness is belied by situations of sadness, loss, death, and oppression.

In a story not found in *St. Rocque* ("On the Bayou Bridge," Vol. 3, WADN), Dunbar-Nelson describes the Bayou St. John:

> In its dark bosom many secrets lie buried. It is like some beautiful serpent, langurous, sinister. It ripples in the sunshine, sparkles in the moonlight, glooms in the dusk and broods in the dark. But it thinks unceasingly, and below its brightest sparkle you feel its unknown soul.

Her stories work in this way. Looking upon them (too) closely, "you would shudder because you feel what lies beneath the brown waters." In *St. Rocque*, the dark Manuela resorts to a voodoo madam to vanquish her blonde rival in romance; Tony's wife is beaten and kicked out on the street; Annette gives up her operatic ambitions after being misled by the fisherman of Pass Christian; dire economic want forces M'sieu Fortier to sell his beloved violin; Athanasia's story becomes yet another "broken-hearted romance" by the Bayou St. John; Sylves', a young Cajun man, is brought back to his fond Maman and fiancé Louisette dead in his coffin after working a winter in Chicago; and thus one could continue.

Beyond these plots, one notes that Dunbar-Nelson is inclined to write about difference—for example, Catholic versus Protestant, Anglo versus Creole. Grandpère Colomes is shamed when "his petite Juanita, his Spanish blossom, his hope of a family that had held itself proudly aloof from 'dose Americain' from time immemorial," smiles "upon this Mercer, this pale-eyed youth." More deeply still, one encounters disturbing tropes of enclosure (the veil, the closing door) which subtly critique female confinement and lack of options. Polysemous texts like "Sister Josepha" (Vol. 1, WADN) and "The Locket" (published outside of *St. Rocque*; Vol. 3, WADN), quasiconventional convent stories, further indict the patriarchal oppression of young girls. Obviously, for the readers of these tales, suffering was romantic—as it has often been taken to be, especially when the sufferer is someone other than oneself.

After *The Goodness of St. Rocque*, Dunbar-Nelson continued to mine Creole materials, but went far beyond the ostensibly safe mode of that volume. The undercurrent of "dark-blooded passion" hinted at in *St. Rocque* erupts into the murderous heroine of "On the Bayou Bridge," whose "long fingers" wind themselves around her abandoning lover's neck "like steel cords." Anglo prejudice becomes overt racism in "Natalie" when Olivia's mother opposes the friendship of her white daughter and the brown maiden Natalie, who has been treated before this incident with "supercilious indifference" or "contemptuous patronage." Most significantly of all, Dunbar-Nelson stops dealing with the Creole as a racial monolith and addresses the specific dilemma of the black Creole who has immediate or identifiable Negro ancestry.

"The Pearl in the Oyster" is one such story, but "The Stones of the Village" is weightier (both stories appear in Vol. 3, WADN). Young Victor Grabért's childhood has been blighted by his ambiguous racial identity. His loving, but stern, old West Indian grandmother forbids him social interaction with the youngsters on his street (whom she vehemently calls "dose niggers").

> It had been loneliness ever since. For the parents of the little black and yellow boys resenting the insult Grandmére had offered their offspring, sternly bade them have nothing more to do with Victor. Then when he toddled after some other little boys, whose faces were white like his own, they ran him away with derisive hoots of "Nigger! Nigger!" And again, he could not understand. . . . [A]ll the boys, white and black and yellow hooted at him and called him "White nigger! White nigger!"

Furthermore, Grandmére forces him to cease speaking "the soft, Creole patois that they chattered together" and learn English, the result being "a confused jumble which was no language at all." This "confused jumble," this silence— linguistic, racial, psychic, and emotional—determines his entire life.

A chain of circumstances cuts off Victor from his past, and he becomes a highly successful lawyer and judge, marries into a leading (white) family, and fathers a fine son. Yet the fear of racial exposure torments him and eventually ends in psychosis, madness, and death. He dies apoplectically, about to address a political banquet, imagining that the men who crowd around to help him are "all boys with stones to pelt him because he wanted to play with them."

In this story, Dunbar-Nelson handles complexities she never touched any place else. Certainly, she is treating the popular Afro-American literary themes of the "color line"— that is, passing—and the "tragic mulatto" from the unique vantage of the Louisiana black Creole. That this troubled subject has autobiographical resonance is clear when it is compared with an essay she wrote around 1929. Entitled "Brass Ankles Speaks" (Vol. 2, WADN), it is an outspoken denunciation of darker skinned black people's prejudice against light-skinned blacks told by a "brass ankles," a black person "white enough to pass for white, but with a darker family back-ground, a real love for the mother race, and no desire to be numbered among the white race." This brass ankles recalls her "miserable" childhood in "a far Southern city" where other schoolchildren taunted and plagued her because she was a "light nigger, with straight hair!" This kind of rebuff and persecution continued into a Northern college and her first teaching job:

> Small wonder, then, that the few lighter persons in the community drew together; we were literally thrown upon each other, whether we liked or not. But when we began going about together and spending time in each other's society, a howl went up. We were organizing a "blue vein" society. We were mistresses of white men. We were Lesbians. We hated black folk and plotted against them. As a matter of fact, we had no other recourse but to cling together.

And she states further that "To complain would be only to bring upon themselves another storm of abuse and fury."

This essay was as close as Dunbar-Nelson ever got to revealing feelings about her own racial status as a "yaller nigger." She tried to publish it, but would not or could not do so under her own name, and the magazine editor refused to print it pseudonymously. "The Stones of the Village" is, likewise, as close as she ever got to turning this kind of personal and cultural confusion into art. One notes, though, that in the story, she uses a male rather than a female protagonist, thereby making it easier to write and keep at a safer distance from herself.

Uncollected stories such as this one are serious, potentially threatening. Consequently, they did not sell easily and many were never published. During the years (1898–1902) of professional authorship when she was the lesser known, female half of the Dunbar writing duo, one of the concrete perquisites of her position was sharing the literary agent Paul Reynolds. Her letters to him show that she kept him supplied with a steady stream of material, much of which came back to her. Those stories of hers that "some of the leading magazines of the country regularly print[ed]"[3] tended to be fluffy romances, often with local color backdrops. To Bliss Perry of *The Atlantic Monthly*, she proposed expanding "The Stones of the Village" into a novel. In an August 22, 1900, reply, he offered his opinion that at present the American public had a "dislike" for treatment of "the color-line." And "Stones" remained in manuscript. Knowing more of these previously unpublished stories would certainly have modified our simple generalizations about Alice Dunbar-Nelson.

This becomes even truer when two other of her stories are considered—"Elisabeth" and "Ellen Fenton" (both appear in

Vol. 3, WADN). With ten additional works, they were to be included in a volume, *Women and Men,* which Dunbar-Nelson projected sometime around 1902. Elisabeth is a thirty-year-old single woman who abruptly finds herself alone in New York City needing to make a living: "I am too old to think about marrying, and too young to go to the poorhouse. . . . Too ugly to be attractive, and not ugly enough to make a living in a sideshow." Her efforts to find a job prove "a lonely struggle, lonely and hard" and the one she finally secures "paid little." Here Dunbar-Nelson begins to explore the psyche and life of an ordinary, post-Victorian working woman. Elisabeth is not rich. She is not a Creole exotic. She is not exemplary in any way.

Ellen Fenton, likewise, wakes up one morning and finds herself unaccountably dissatisfied with her forty years of living: "Something was whirling within her, an indefinable feeling that she too, wanted to say aloud . . . 'I don't want to do the same thing; I want to do something different.' " She has been a model wife and mother, a civic inspiration, but now she begins to brood and change until she makes a startling discovery:

> She had always been a woman, who in addition to the multiple cares of her household and public philanthropy, to use the cant phrase, "lived her own life." She was discovering now that the term was a misnomer. The average woman, she found, who "lives her own life," in reality, lives others', and has no life of her own.

Today, this reads like an early formulation of "the feminine mystique"—and indeed would have been had Dunbar-Nelson stuck with her gender analysis and not "universalized" the issue by also giving Ellen's husband Herbert a parallel midlife crisis. Similarly, she sidesteps original exploration of Elisabeth's dilemma by turning her story into a happily-ever-after romance. In both cases, her "modern feminist realism" (a phrase Alain Locke used in commenting upon Georgia Douglas Johnson, Edna St. Vincent Millay, and Sara Teasdale)[4] is wrenched into submission and never fully realized.

This realism burgeons into urban naturalism in *The Annals of 'Steenth Street* (Vol. 3, WADN), another projected volume of short stories. These stories build on the experience Dunbar-Nelson gained doing settlement work and teaching on New York City's East Side in 1897–1898. 'Steenth Street is her "Main Street," located around 87th between Second and Third Avenues, underneath the El with the East River in view. The protagonists of these tales are Irish ghetto youth whom the reader comes to know as they appear throughout the collection—Abe Powers, James Brown, Scrappy Franks, Dobson, Hattie Gurton, Della Mott, Lizzie Williams, Gus Schwartz. Perhaps Dunbar-Nelson saw these narratives as juvenile fiction, a possibility that is suggested by the fact that one of the two stories from this set that were published, "The Revenge of James Brown," appeared as a Methodist Episcopal Church young people's story in 1929. Again perhaps, this fictional vehicle may have been chosen because it helped to present the harsh social criticism inherent in the selections in a more harmless guise.

The denizens of this neighborhood live hard lives. Money is short or nonexistent, the next meal is a daily problem, parents are alcoholics, and drunken fathers beat their stepdaughters. In the midst of all this, a guy must save face with the gang, a girl needs a dress for the ball of a lifetime, a rival wins favor for peanuts, and women like Mrs. McMahon pick up the pieces when the makeshift foundations crumble. Dunbar-Nelson sees with analytical clarity the female lot. When Belle finally kills her deserving husband ("Witness for the Defense," Vol. 3, WADN), 'Steenth Street celebrates:

> For so long had woman-kind in this particular section of the world quietly taken its beatings, gone without food or fire or light, while its better half found all three with amusement and jollity thrown in at McEneny's on the corner; . . . for so long had the survival of the strongest been the implacable law that now when one woman had broken the bonds of custom and established the right to live and to kill too, there was great rejoicing. The women stood about in doorways and halls and discussed the event with avidity. Emancipation was in the air.

Dunbar-Nelson is also sensitive to the plight of the children. Abe Powers ("The Downfall of Abe Powers," Vol. 3, WADN) writes to the mission matron:

> "Dere Miss Morton, I beat Mr. coller an put him out becos he talked too much an i dont see why we has to be bothered when our mothers is drunk an if you will plese forgive me an let me come to the [Christmas] tree i will be gode. . ."

The stories are about oppression. The idea of difference, which always interested Dunbar-Nelson, becomes here class difference. This she uses, I am sure, as a signifier for race. The vocabulary of racism is unmistakable in Miss Tillman's language ("Miss Tillman's Protege," Vol. 3, WADN) when she breathes raptures about adopting little Hattie: "Such a dear, sweet, patient face. She'd look lovely in a dear white apron with her hair smooth sitting at my feet in my study." When Mrs. Morton reminds her that Hattie may have "family ties, and a mother," she counters, "it's absurd. These people are very different from us. I thought you knew that from your long experience with them."

The kind of transmutations occurring in these stories is further suggested when they are compared with Dunbar-Nelson's comments in a January 23, 1898, letter to her fiancé Paul. She reported a visit to the home of one of her students, where she found a German woman married to a "shiftless, dirty Negro" who drank, beat, and neglected her and the children. They were about to be evicted from two smelly, squalid rooms, had no coal, no food, a nursing baby, a toddler with chicken pox, etc. The scene gets shifted straight into the 'Steenth Street fiction, with only the "shiftless, dirty Negro" bleached out. Why? One reason is that Dunbar-Nelson did not wish to portray this type of black person. Other reasons may relate to marketing conditions, her authorial psychology, and the tricky *why*s and *wherefore*s of her literary passing game. ("Hope Deferred" [Vol. 3, WADN] is an exception in her fictional corpus.)

Nowhere is the sense of passing greater than in her specifically autobiographical stories, those few pieces where she takes herself and the details of her experience as material. It could also be said that nowhere would the need for camouflage be as crucial. Yet one wonders what Dunbar-Nelson thought she could have been concealing. Any of these stories published under her own name would have functioned like public monologues to a voyeuristic analyst. This accounts for her use of a pseudonym and also for the fact that at least one of them reads more like a therapeutic piece of personal catharsis than a work she intended to publish.

Three stories (Vol. 3, WADN) fall into this category—"Mrs. Newly-wed and Her Servants," "The Decision," and

"No Sacrifice." Interestingly, all of them reflect her relationship with Paul Laurence Dunbar. "Mrs. Newly-wed" does so in an innocuous manner, since it is a doleful tale of a freshly married young wife reciting to her amused but sympathetic friend the problems she has had with a long roll of unsatisfactory female servants. She is Alice as Mrs. Paul Laurence Dunbar, after the couple set up housekeeping in Washington, D.C., casting herself into yet another role. "The Decision" and "No Sacrifice" are barely veiled accounts of Alice's courtship and marriage with Paul. Here is a trove of accurate information about their meeting through a magazine, becoming impulsively engaged before Paul sails overseas, Alice's mother's disapproval, their romantic passion and stormy public fights, his bouts with alcohol, her refusal to visit him on his sick bed, and all the rest that made their union romantic copy for scandalmongers. A reader familiar with the relationship peruses these stories for clues to answer the questions of what went wrong and why Alice so obdurately refused to be reconciled.

This aspect of the works aside, their next most striking feature is the way that Dunbar-Nelson has made the narratives racially white. Mrs. Newly-wed recruits her help from the "camp," "that disreputable part of the town just below the Sixth Street hill where a lot of colored folks have congregated." When he is intoxicated, Burt Courtland's eyes are "red-streaked across their blue." Gerald Kennedy is a "Greek God" with "chestnut hair" whose emotional face "flares crimson." Furthermore, wealth abounds. Burt has built Marion a "great, dreary new mansion," the couples "jet-set" like Scott and Zelda Fitzgerald, rich uncles die leaving behind their millions. This lavish flow of dollars calls to mind Dunbar-Nelson saying that play money figured so prominently on stage in black drama because the real thing was such a scarce commodity in actual life (a circumstance that was true for her until the end of her days). Seemingly, too, for Dunbar-Nelson, white equalled rich (or was it that rich equalled white?)—unless fate landed one on 'Steenth Street.

So much of these stories is fact-based fantasy ("No Sacrifice" was written as a "True Story") that it is hard to think through (and beyond) this component—and in the works themselves, images of falseness and illusion are prevalent. Ultimately, these texts reveal the author's attempt to write about herself—but from deep within limiting psychic and formal structures.

Dunbar-Nelson rounded out her short-story career with snappily written pieces in the newly emerging American detective genre. It is not surprising that she would find this "hard-boiled" tradition attractive since the no-nonsense, rational "tough guy" was one of her private personae—and also because she often tried her hand at whatever was new and modern and promised financial reward. A vacationing private detective lays the foundation for the surprise ending of "His Great Career," while "Summer Session" shows us Mr. Terence McShane nabbing the criminal (a white slavery perpetrator) and then winning the girl, to boot. Both stories are slick, well-made; but there is no evidence that they were ever published (Vol. 3, WADN).

Dunbar-Nelson wrote many stories not included here in *The Works of Alice Dunbar-Nelson* and, at her death, left behind both typescripts and holograph drafts. From the publication of *Violets* through the early 1900s, short stories received her most concentrated attention. And as late as 1928, a newspaper article reported that she "considers her short stories her most representative work."[5] Certainly, taken as a whole, this fiction is impressively various and surprisingly complex.

Dunbar-Nelson also tried longer fiction, writing (or partially writing) at least four novels—*The Confessions of a Lazy Woman* (ca. 1899, cast in diary form); *A Modern Undine* (ca. 1901–1903; Vol. 2, WADN); *Uplift* (1930–1931, intended as a satire of an insincere black woman who professionally represents the race; Dunbar-Nelson destroyed the manuscript because of dissatisfaction with it); and *This Lofty Oak* (1932–1933, the extremely long, fictionalized biography of her friend, Delaware educator Edwina B. Kruse). While she was writing *Uplift,* she derisively referred to it as "the Great American Novel," indicating, I think, both her desire to pen that national classic and her knowledge that she was incapable of doing so.[6]

Of these works, *A Modern Undine* is the most satisfactory and most fully realized. It exists as a seventy-nine-page, typed manuscript that can be justifiably considered an organic novelette since it is Dunbar-Nelson's first, complete draft (stretching plots to standard novel length was always one of her problems). We know that she added some now-lost pages because a professional opinion she received in 1903 objected to the ease with which the heroine finds her lost husband.[7] *Undine* tells the story of Marion, a decorous, self-centered, introverted, prickly-sensitive, twenty-four-year-old Southern woman. From a home made lively by her mother and hoydenish sister, she marries Howard, a Northern businessman who falls in love with her despite her aloofness. Mistakenly thinking that Howard is having an affair with a poor girl in the town, Marion retreats even further into paranoia and obsessive mothering of their crippled son. Everything climaxes at once. The truth about the affair comes out; Howard's business fails in the general crash and he has to flee charges of embezzlement; he and Marion for the first time in their lives speak frankly about their feelings, with Howard openly criticizing her narrowness and self-centeredness. Reading this, one is somehow drawn into the rather strange tale, becoming irritated with Marion's almost-total withdrawal from feelings and the world, sympathizing with Howard, and so on. The psychological dimensions are strong (reflecting Dunbar-Nelson's lifelong fascination with this field).

However, the key to understanding this novelette lies in its title. In folklore, an *undine* is a "female water sprite who could acquire a soul by marrying a human being." But if her lover proved unfaithful, she would have to return to the sea.[8] Marion is this spirit. When we first glimpse her on the night she meets Howard, she is standing on the edge of a breakwater with the sea surging at her feet "in a low monotone of life and death." The second time we see her, she gazes "out at the sea," seeming more than ever "in her curious detachment from her surroundings" to remind Howard of "a vestal set apart from the rest of mankind, awaiting mysterious voices from heaven." Water references and the sea motif continue, especially at critical points in the plot. When she first discovers what she thinks is her husband's infidelity, Marion's fainting is imaged as "the darkness and roaring of the sea clos[ing] over her head." After her baby dies, she directs her mother to "bury him by the sea . . . perhaps it will sing to him the same songs it has sung to me."

Further, in these folkloric terms, Marion's "becoming human" through the vicissitudes of love and marriage is emphatically focused. That she is warped is symbolized in the deformity of her child, who was maimed in her womb when she fainted, and of whom she is jealously possessive. During their climactic argument, Howard rebukes her for fancying herself "too superior to come out of the clouds long enough to touch the vital human things of this world," and tells her that getting involved with charity work "would have made [her] seem more like a human being." Humanity first flares in her when she waits to accuse Howard of visiting his paramour: "A cold, deadly fury was stirring at her heart, becoming more passionate and human at every instant that Howard stayed in the house." At the end of their encounter, "for an instant she felt again strangely aloof from the whole scene, apart and out of the disaster which threatened her whole life, but only for an instant." She has entered the realm of human love and sorrow, in a novel which affirms both.

A Modern Undine reflects the fact that Dunbar-Nelson, an astrological Cancer, loved the sea—and rhapsodized about it in her diary:

> But the water! . . . Weeks I dreamed of it. . . . No inconvenience too great for the love of it. . . Lovely, luxurious, voluptuous water.[9]

Deeper still, the work reveals her connection with myth, the mystical, and the spiritual. Her daily living envinced an awareness of meta-realms of experience beyond the visible world which was rooted in her mother's Obeah beliefs and enhanced by her own attention to the spiritual arts. This seems to be the level of reality she is adumbrating here—and is the only time this mystical consciousness is specifically developed in her literary work.

On a completely different plane, it can be noted that, more than once, Dunbar-Nelson wrote about an uninvolved female. *The Confessions of a Lazy Woman*—ultimately a rather silly work—features a heroine who strives (and she really has to work at it) to do absolutely nothing. Dunbar-Nelson was just the opposite, what she herself once described as "another too-busy woman." Might this imaging of idleness and withdrawal be wish fulfillment of a more significant kind than that represented by the material wealth of her romances? It may be that these figures represent—simultaneously—a longing for and a critique of female passivity/inactivity/worldly isolation (they don't even read the newspaper). As a critique, they present the feminine ideal elevated to the satiric nth degree of foolishness.

Thinking in this way raises the comparison between Dunbar-Nelson and her female protagonists. Not one of them is even remotely like her. Unfortunately, when she tried to transcribe her own self/body in the autobiographical romances, the attempts were unsuccessful at best and disastrous at worst. None of her heroines are black—no Iola Leroy or Megda or some other figure to carry us forward to Helga Crane or Janie Starks. One wonders, if they had been black, could Dunbar-Nelson have done a better, or different, job with them? A black woman like herself on the printed page in 1915 would have been a sight to behold. What she did (and did not do) with *Uplift* and *This Lofty Oak* suggests that black women's lives (her own and others') were too real to be fiction—as she understood fiction to be in those largely premodernist days. And there was simply too much that she did not want to say about herself. All of this is, of course, speculation; Dunbar-Nelson did what she could and we can try to understand and appreciate that, even as we wish for more.

What she was able to achieve in prose outweighs her poetic accomplishments although, ironically, being taken as a poet has helped immensely to keep her reputation alive. Dunbar-Nelson was not driven to write poems and did not focus on the genre. When asked by an editor for a poem in 1900, she confessed to being short on poetic inspiration and added,

"Mr. Dunbar tells me that I average one poem in six months, and that there will be none due for several weeks to come." [10] If anything, Paul's estimate is a bit high when spread over her lifetime of writing.

By and large, Dunbar-Nelson's poetry (included in Vol. 2, WADN) is what it appears to be—competent treatments of conventional lyric themes in traditional forms and styles. Her signature poem, "Violets," is the apogee of this type. A few others stand out for various reasons. "I Sit and Sew," wherein a woman chafes at her domestic role during wartime, seems feminist in spirit. "You! Inez!" appears to be a rare eruption in verse of Dunbar-Nelson's lesbian feelings. "Communion" and "Music" were probably (like "Violets") selections in a no longer extant *Dream Book* commemorating her illicit affair with Emmett J. Scott, Jr. "To Madame Curie" and "Cano—I Sing" are strikingly well executed. "April Is On the Way" is a confusingly complicated work about a rape (or attempted rape) and lynching. "Forest Fire" shows Dunbar-Nelson trying to modernize her technique during the Harlem Renaissance years of experimentation. "The Proletariat Speaks" reminds one of her consciousness about difference and class contrasts. "Little Roads" contains a pun on "Fay," the name of the woman with whom she was romantically involved when she wrote it in 1930–1931. "Harlem John Henry Views the Airmada" is an "epic of Negro Peace" complete with a black protagonist and slave spirituals.

Though Dunbar-Nelson's poetry improves markedly from her juvenile verse to the mature work of the 1920s, her gifts—which were more discursive than poetic—were not geared in that direction. Furthermore, her essentially romantic conception of poetry caused her to reserve it for intense emotion and other special occasions. Yet it was one more way that she proved herself a writer and solidified her stature as such.

This same statement can be made about her drama, with the clarification that her interest in this genre may have been keener. From her girlhood in New Orleans, Dunbar-Nelson participated in amateur theater. She was also an avid play (and movie) goer, and she wrote and directed plays and pageants for school and community groups. In the Afro-American community, skits and plays for class night programs, for Christmas and Easter church celebrations, and for club fundraising attractions have always been important. Thus, this form was very much a part of Dunbar-Nelson's personal and cultural background. It also suited her often dramatic (not to say theatrical) temperament.

Furthermore, the early twentieth-century black cultural debates often eddied around the drama. The explosion of dark faces on Broadway (notably in the musicals of the 1920s) was paralleled by the development of serious drama in predominantly black colleges (Howard University in Washington, D.C., was a major center) and the proliferation of plays about blacks by famous white playwrights (Eugene O'Neill's *Emperor Jones* was perhaps the most celebrated). At the same time, Oscar Michaeux and a few others were pioneering the race film and black movie making. Something of this ferment can be picked up in Dunbar-Nelson's newspaper columns. It was a time of intense pronouncements about the proper portrayal of the Negro on stage. A 1928 newspaper article uncovers Dunbar-Nelson adding her bit to the current dialogue:

> [Dunbar-Nelson] believes that the stage is the best medium for exploiting ourselves; that we must break away from

propaganda per se and the conventional musical comedy that
starts on a plantation and ends in a cabaret, and present to
the American public all phases of Negro life and culture.[11]

This contextual grounding of her plays in black life probably helps account for Dunbar-Nelson's use in them of iden-
tifiably black characters, settings, and situations (which is
unlike her fiction). Then, too, this would have to be the case
if she had any intention at all of seeing them performed. The
same 1928 article also mentioned that she "preferred" writing
plays (though one cannot fathom what that really means,
given her literary record) and had done "a number" of them
for "amateur producers." Her extant works for her Howard
High School groups are obviously designed for the educa-
tional and moral edification of the students. Something like
the *Club Ritz-Carlton,* a cabaret show that she staged for the
Wilmington, Delaware, Elk Daughters, can only be conjec-
tured about. Her most well-known and probably most acted
play was *Mine Eyes Have Seen* (Vol. 3, WADN; publication
in the *Crisis* helped its visibility). There is no evidence that
the others included here (Vol. 3, WADN) were ever mounted.

Question: What kind of black folk does Dunbar-Nelson
present in her racial plays? On the whole, they are all
recognizable types—as dramatic characters are traditionally
wont to be. In *Mine Eyes,* Lucy is the gentle, patient sister
who takes care of her two motherless brothers; Cornelia Lewis
is a conscientious settlement worker; Dan is the older brother
literally crippled by racial prejudice. *Gone White* (Vol. 3,
WADN) highlights Allan Franklin Cordell, a light-skinned,
young, educated black man determined to compel potential
employers "to admit that a Negro can be as good or better
an engineer than a white man," to "ram their damn prejudice

down their throats." Granny Wimbish moans spirituals, and
Anna Martin is as long-serving as Lucy. Blanche Parker,
Allan's aunt, strikes a more original note. Frankly (even
immorally) pragmatic, she puts Allan through college (by
dressing hair in her own beauty shop), then counsels him to
pass for white and maintain his white wife, family, and
position, and—if he must—"love" his brown-skinned Anna
on the side. Though mostly poor, the characters are decent,
respectable, and above all, well-spoken. There is no dialect
here, no comedy, as Dunbar-Nelson tries to live up to her
call for a broader, more realistic Afro-American drama.

The fact that these plays treat controversial topics helped
Dunbar-Nelson achieve more intense effects. *Mine Eyes* argues for blacks to support World War I, but presents the
glaring contradictions. When Chris is drafted, he asks, "Must
I go and fight for the nation that let my father's murder [by
whites] go unpunished? That killed my mother—that took
away my chances for making a man out of myself?" And in
Gone White when Anna comprehends what Allan wants, she
"speaks through clenched teeth":

> You are offering me the position of your mistress. . . . You
> would keep your white wife, and all that that means, for
> respectability's sake—but you would have a romance, a liaison
> with the brown woman whom you love, after dark. No Negro
> could stoop so low as to take on such degraded ideals of so-
> called racial purity. And this is the moral deterioration to
> which you have brought your whole race. White Man! Go
> on back to your white gods! Lowest and vilest of scum. White
> Man! Go Back!

The Author's Evening at Home and *Love's Disguise*, a silent
film scenario (both in Vol. 3, WADN), round out the view
of Dunbar-Nelson in the dramatic media. The first work,

really a 1900 playlet, is a slick piece that capitalizes on her relationship with Paul. The credit line in *Smart Set* read "By Alice Dunbar (Mrs. Paul Laurence Dunbar)" and suggested a real-life genesis for this comedy about an author in his library who cannot write because of his disruptive wife and mother. *Love's Disguise*—with its extreme portrayal of duality—is simply an instance of Dunbar-Nelson's flirtation with silent filmscripts. Eventually, she gave up the notion and concentrated her talent in forms more feasible for her.

This completes the survey of Dunbar-Nelson's work in the canonical genres. She also did a large amount of other writing that is just as important. In it (her essays, for example), she is as relentlessly racial as she is nonracial in the fine genres, suggesting, of course, that her concepts of genre-reality-race were rigidly stratified. Furthermore, it is in this nonbelle-tristic work that she truly inscribes herself. Nowhere is this more evident than in her diary, which she kept during 1921 and 1926–1931. Here she allows herself to star, center stage in all her complexity and beauty. Even though no excerpts are included in this collection because this journal is easily available, it is an indispensable portion of her works.[12]

The "real" Dunbar-Nelson also "stands up" in her newspaper columns, playing the role of the urbane journalist—a pose that superbly suited her as individual and artist. This liberating stance permitted her to be as contrary and self-contradictory as she wished. A mobile, moody thinker, she could say one thing on Saturday and something completely different the next week. The column form likewise allowed for variation in length and emphasis ranging from one-liners and snippets to full-scale, expository essays. In any case, Dunbar-Nelson consistently spoke out "from a (black) woman's point of view" (as she did, too, in essays such as "Facing Life Squarely" [Vol. 2, WADN] with its memorable observation that "the spectacle of two or three ordinary Southern white women sitting down to talk with several very high class black women" does not represent racial progress worth "sobbing with joy" about). However, what she wrote was definitely not a typical "woman's" column devoted to narrowly defined feminine concerns.

Even after sixty years, her weekly pieces are very readable and engaging—which is praise indeed for writing produced as ephemera. The intellect, wit, protest, sassiness, iconoclasm, racial pride, feminism, and humor that one yearns for in her fictional heroines can all be found here. These columns have to be read to be appreciated, and some of their impact is cumulative (like the diary). In her April 10, 1926 "Une Femme Dit" (Vol. 2, WADN), Dunbar-Nelson repeats an accolade:

> Mrs. Myrtle Foster Cook, the charming and gracile editor of the *National Notes*, the official organ of the National Association of Colored Women, says that this column is "as delectable and refreshing as a cool lemonade after a hectic day."
>
> That is delightful praise. Should one be too modest to reproduce it? Not so. Modesty went out with the corset, the pompadour, long skirts, lined dresses, the knitted petticoat, the merry widow hat, the lisle stocking, the chatelaine bag, and the fleur de lys watch pin. Indeed, so much is modesty a lost art, that one is almost tempted to repeat the entire paragraph from the *National Notes*. But lingering phases of reluctance, delicate and obscure, forbid. We rise and make our best bow in the direction of Kansas City

—while "we" blow our nails and polish them on the bodice of our dress, in that stage business of self-satisfied modesty whose verbal approximation is "ahem." Mrs. Cook is backed up—though in sexist fashion—by Eugene Gordon, who wrote this of Dunbar-Nelson in a 1927 *Opportunity* magazine "Survey of the Negro Press": "In my estimation there are few better column conductors of her sex on any newspaper. I should like to see her on some influential daily where her unmistakable talents would be allowed full exercise." [13]

"Une Femme Dit"—which began as "From A Woman's Point of View," and which shows Dunbar-Nelson at her best—was written for the Pittsburgh *Courier* from February 20, 1926, to September 18, 1926. "As In a Looking Glass" (Vol. 2, WADN) appeared in the Washington *Eagle* from 1926 to 1930. (Dunbar-Nelson also wrote another column, "So It Seems—to Alice Dunbar-Nelson," for the *Courier* from January to May 1930, but this series betrays some diminution of verve and interest.) In these columns (of which the selection in Vol. 2 represents only a small part), Dunbar-Nelson shines as literary critic, political analyst, social commentator, race theorist, humorist, and stage and film critic. During this age of print journalism and rising syndicated chains, when newspaper work was a man's profession, Dunbar-Nelson felt that pressure but excelled nonetheless.

It is unfortunate that this writing, which contains so much of her creative energy, is so underrated as art. Valorizing these texts is the most radical example of the re-reading of Alice Dunbar-Nelson which I hope this edition of her works will foster.

NOTES

1. For a fuller treatment of Alice Dunbar-Nelson's life and more information about her writings, see the chapter devoted to her in

Gloria T. Hull, *Color, Sex, and Poetry: Three Women Writers of the Harlem Renaissance* (Bloomington: Indiana University Press, 1987). Some material in this introduction is taken from this source.

2. Pittsburgh *Christian Advocate,* December 21, 1899.

3. "Mrs. Paul Laurence Dunbar, Wife of the Colored Poet and Novelist," Chicago *Recorder,* August 4, 1902.

4. Alain Locke, "Foreword" to Georgia Douglas Johnson, *An Autumn Love Cycle* (New York: Harold Vinal, Ltd., 1928), p. xviii.

5. Newspaper clipping, no name, July 4, 1928. From the vertical file of the Schomburg Center for Research in Black Culture, New York City.

6. Dunbar-Nelson's diary for 1930–1931 charts her writing of *Uplift.* See Gloria T. Hull (ed.), *Give Us Each Day: The Diary of Alice Dunbar-Nelson* (New York: W. W. Norton, 1984).

7. J. N. M. (?) to Alice Dunbar-Nelson, July 16, 1903. For this "expert opinion," Dunbar-Nelson paid five dollars.

8. Information taken from William H. Harris and Judith S. Levey (eds.), *The New Columbia Encyclopedia* (New York: Columbia University Press, 1975), p. 2822.

9. Hull (ed.), *Give Us Each Day,* p. 325.

10. The New York City *Chute* (?), May 1900.

11. Unidentified July 4, 1928 clipping from the Schomburg Center vertical file.

12. Bibliographical data cited in note 6 above.

13. Quoted as an epigraph to Dunbar-Nelson's February 25, 1927, "As In a Looking Glass" column.

EDITORIAL NOTE

Bibliographic information for Alice Dunbar-Nelson's published work, when known, is noted at the beginning of each text. Unpublished manuscripts can be found in the Special Collections of the Morris Library, University of Delaware, Newark, Delaware. Prior to this present edition, R. Ora Williams helped to make Dunbar-Nelson's work somewhat more available in her *An Alice Dunbar-Nelson Reader* (Washington, D.C.: University Press of America, Inc., 1979). She also published "Works By and About Alice Ruth (Moore) Dunbar-Nelson: A Bibliography" in the *CLA Journal*, XIX, No. 3 (March, 1976). Both of these are useful references.

For this edition of Dunbar-Nelson's works, it was clear that her two published books should be reprinted. In selecting the other works, I used the criteria of autobiographical and literary interest, artistic merit, and representativeness, while keeping in mind the space available. Including the 595 typed manuscript pages of *This Lofty Oak* did not seem compellingly feasible or worthwhile. Nor did I choose to collect a greater number of her slighter romantic stories. Likewise, high school plays and pageants were not considered important enough for publication, but all of her apparently finished, available poetry is here.

Her articles and essays for outlets like *The Southern Workman*, *The Messenger*, and the *Journal of Negro History* are least represented. Though valuable, they are standard expository and argumentative pieces written in an objective style, which makes them not as vital as Dunbar-Nelson's other noncanonical work for understanding her life and art. However, what they do sharpen is the dichotomy between the nonracialness of her belletristic genres and the racialness of her other writings. The inclusions from her newspaper columns were probably made most impressionistically (and were also influenced by whether the originals were crumbling or had been photocopied). Given what they are, reading through any runs of them provides very similar materials and insights.

The selections are presented here as Dunbar-Nelson wrote them, with only obvious typographical and spelling errors corrected.

ALICE DUNBAR-NELSON

A CHRONOLOGY

1875	July 19, born in New Orleans, Louisiana.
1892	Graduated from Straight College, New Orleans; subsequently studied at Cornell, Columbia, the Pennsylvania School of Industrial Art, and the University of Pennsylvania, specializing in English educational measurements and psychology.
1892–1896	Taught school in New Orleans.
1895	Published *Violets and Other Tales* (Boston: The Monthly Review Press)—short stories and poems.
1897–1898	Taught in Brooklyn, New York; helped to found the White Rose Mission, which became the White Rose Home for Girls in Harlem.
1898	March 8, married poet Paul Laurence Dunbar and began living in Washington, D.C.
1899	Published *The Goodness of St. Rocque and Other Stories* (New York: Dodd, Mead, and Co.)—short stories.
1902	Separated from Paul Laurence Dunbar and moved to Wilmington, Delaware (he died February 6, 1906).
1902–1920	Taught and administered at the Howard High School, Wilmington; for seven of these years, also directed the summer sessions for in-

This chronology appeared in Gloria T. Hull (ed.), *Give Us Each Day: The Diary of Alice Dunbar-Nelson*. New York: W. W. Norton, 1984.

	service teachers at State College for Colored Students (now Delaware State College), Dover; and taught two years in the summer session at Hampton Institute.
1909	April, published "Wordsworth's Use of Milton's Description of Pandemonium" in *Modern Language Notes*.
1910	January 19, married teacher Henry Arthur Callis secretly in Wilmington. He left the next year for medical school in Chicago. (They were later divorced at some unknown time.)
1913–1914	Wrote for and helped edit the *A.M.E. Church Review*.
1914	Edited and published *Masterpieces of Negro Eloquence* (Harrisburg, Pennsylvania: The Douglass Publishing Company).
1915	Was field organizer for the Middle Atlantic States in the campaign for women's suffrage.
1916	April 20, married Robert J. Nelson, a journalist.
1916–1917	Published a two-part article, "People of Color in Louisiana," in *The Journal of Negro History*.
1917–1928	Published poems in *Crisis, Ebony and Topaz, Opportunity, Negro Poets and Their Poems, Caroling Dusk, The Dunbar Speaker and Entertainer, Harlem: A Forum of Negro Life*, etc.
1918	Toured the South as a field representative of the Woman's Committee of the Council of National Defense.

1920	Served on the State Republican Committee of Delaware and directed political activities among black women; edited and published *The Dunbar Speaker and Entertainer* (Naperville, Illinois: J. L. Nichols and Co.); drawing on her interests in juvenile delinquency and "abnormal psychology," worked with women from the State Federation of Colored Women to found the Industrial School for Colored Girls in Marshalltown, Delaware.
1920–1922	Coedited and published the Wilmington *Advocate* newspaper.
1921	August, began her *Diary* and kept an extant portion of it for the remainder of the year.
1922	Headed the Anti-Lynching Crusaders in Delaware fighting for the Dyer Anti-Lynching Bill.
1924	Directed the Democratic political campaign among black women from New York headquarters; August and September, published a two-part article on Delaware in "These 'Colored' United States" in *The Messenger*.
1924–1928	Was teacher and parole officer at the Industrial School for Colored Girls.
1926	January 2–September 18, wrote column "From A Woman's Point of View" (later changed to "Une Femme Dit") in the Pittsburgh *Courier*.
1926–1930	Wrote column "As In a Looking Glass" in the Washington *Eagle* (her columns and/or versions of them were also syndicated for the Associated Negro Press).

1926–1931   Resumed and kept the remaining extant portions of her *Diary*.

1928–1931   Was executive secretary of the American Friends Inter-Racial Peace Committee, which entailed much travel and public speaking.

1930   January–May, wrote column "So It Seems to Alice Dunbar-Nelson" in the Pittsburgh *Courier*.

1931   Included in James Weldon Johnson's *The Book of American Negro Poetry*.

1932   Moved to Philadelphia, after Robert was appointed to the Pennsylvania Athletic (Boxing) Commission in January.

1935   September 18, died of heart trouble at the University of Pennsylvania Hospital. She was cremated in Wilmington and her ashes eventually scattered over the Delaware River.

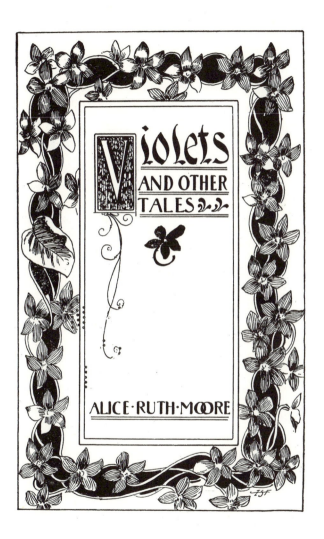

Violets

AND OTHER TALES

ALICE · RUTH · MOORE

To my friend of November 5th, 1892

INTRODUCTION.

In this day when the world is fairly teeming with books,— good books, books written with a motive, books inculcating morals, books teaching lessons,—it seems almost a piece of presumption too great for endurance to foist another upon the market. There is scarcely room in the literary world for amateurs and maiden efforts; the very worthiest are sometimes poorly repaid for their best efforts. Yet, another one is offered the public, a maiden effort,— a little thing with absolutely nothing to commend it, that seeks to do nothing more than amuse.

Many of these sketches and verses have appeared in print before, in newspapers and a magazine or two; many are seeing the light of day for the first time. If perchance this collection of idle thoughts may serve to while away an hour or two, or lift for a brief space the load of care from someone's mind, their purpose has been served — the author is satisfied.

A. R. M.

CONTENTS.

PREFACE.

These fugitive pieces are launched upon the tide of public opinion to sink or swim upon their merit. They will float for a while, but whether they will reach the haven of popularity depends upon their enduring qualities. Some will surely perish, many will reach some port, but time alone will tell if any shall successfully breast the ocean of thought and plant its standard upon the summit of fame.

When one enters the domain of authorship, she places herself at the mercy of critics. Were she as sure of being commended by the best and most intelligent of her readers, as she is sure of being condemned by the worst and most ignorant, there would still be a thrill of pleasure in all criticism, for the satisfaction of having received the praise of the first would compensate for the harshness of the latter. Just criticism is wholesome and never wounds the sensibilities of the true author, for it saves her from the danger of an excess of pride which is the greatest foe to individual progress, while it spurs her on to loftier flights and nobler deeds. A poor writer is bad, but a poor critic is worse, thefore, unjust criticism should never ruffle the temper of its victim. The author of these pages belongs to that type of the "brave new woman who scorns to sigh," but feels that she has something to say, and says it to the best of her ability, and leaves the verdict in the hands of the public. She gives to the reader her best thoughts and leaves him to accept or reject as merit may manifest itself. No author is under contract to please her readers at all times, nor can she hope to con-trol the sentiments of all of them at any time, therefore, the obligation is reciprocal, for the fame she receives is due to the pleasure she af-fords.

The author of these fugitive pieces is young, just on the threshold of life, and with the daring audacity of youth makes assertions and gives decisions which she may reverse as time mellows her opinions, and the realities of life force aside the theories of youth, and prosy facts obscure the memory of that happy time when the heart overflowing with ——

"The joy
.Of young ideas painted on the mind,
In the warm glowing colors Fancy spreads
On objects, not yet known, when all is new,
And all is lovely."

There is much in this book that is good ; much

that is crude; some that is poor: but all give that assurance of something great and noble when the bud of promise, now unfolding its petals in the morning glow of light, will have matured into that fuller growth of blossoming flower ere the noonday sun passes its zenith. May the hope thus engendered by this first attempt reach its fruition, and may the energy displayed by one so young meet the reward it merits from an approving public.

SYLVANIE F. WILLIAMS.

VIOLETS.

I.

"And she tied a bunch of violets with a tress of her pretty brown hair."

She sat in the yellow glow of the lamplight softly humming these words. It was Easter evening, and the newly risen spring world was slowly sinking to a gentle, rosy, opalescent slumber, sweetly tired of the joy which had pervaded it all day. For in the dawn of the perfect morn, it had arisen, stretched out its arms in glorious happiness to greet the Saviour and said its hallelujahs, merrily trilling out carols of bird, and organ and flower-song. But the evening had come, and rest.

There was a letter lying on the table, it read:

"Dear, I send you this little bunch of flowers as my Easter token. Perhaps you may not be able to read their meaning, so I'll tell you. Violets, you know, are my favorite flowers. Dear, little, human-faced things! They seem always as if about to whisper a love-word; and then they signify that thought which passes always between you and me. The orange blossoms—you know their meaning; the little pinks are the flowers you love'; the evergreen leaf is the symbol of the endurance of our affection; the tube-roses I put in, because once when you kissed and pressed me close in your arms, I had a bunch of tube-roses on my bosom, and the heavy fragrance of their crushed loveliness has always lived in my memory. The violets and pinks are from a bunch I wore to-day, and when kneeling at the altar, during communion, did I sin, dear, when I thought of you? The tube-roses and orange-blossoms I wore Friday night; you always wished for a lock of my hair, so I'll tie these flowers with them—but there, it is not stable enough; let me wrap them with a bit of ribbon, pale blue, from that little dress I wore last winter to the dance, when we had such a long, sweet talk in that forgotten nook. You always loved that dress, it fell in such soft ruffles away from the throat and bosom,—you called me your little forget-me-not, that night. I laid the flowers away for awhile in our favorite book,—Byron—just at the poem we loved best, and now I send them to you. Keep them always in remembrance of me, and if aught should occur to sepa-ate us, press these flowers to your lips, and I will be with you in spirit, perme-ating your heart with unutterable love and happiness."

———.

II.

It is Easter again. As of old, the joyous bells clang out the glad news of the resurrection. The giddy, dancing sunbeams laugh riotously in field and street; birds carol their sweet twitterings everywhere, and the heavy perfume of flowers scents the golden atmosphere with inspiring fragrance. One long, golden sunbeam steals silently into the white-curtained window of a quiet room, and lay athwart a sleeping face. Cold, pale, still, its fair, young face pressed against the satin-lined casket. Slender, white fingers, idle now, they that had never known rest; locked softly over a bunch of violets; violets and tube-roses in her soft, brown hair, violets in the bosom of her long, white gown; violets and tube-roses and orange-blossoms banked everywhere, until the air was filled with the ascending souls of the human flowers. Some whispered that a broken heart had ceased to flutte in that still, young form, and that it was a mercy for the soul to ascend on the slender sunbeam. To-day she kneels at the throne of heaven, where one ar ago she had communed at an earthly altar.

III.

Far away in a distant city, a man, carelessly looking among some papers, turned over a faded bunch of flowers tied with a blue ribbon and a lock of hair. He paused meditatively awhile, then turning to the regal-looking woman lounging before the fire, he asked:

"Wife, did you ever send me these?"

She raised her great, black eyes to his with a gesture of ineffable disdain, and replied languidly:

"You know very well I can't bear flowers. How could I ever send such sentimental trash to any one? Throw them into the fire."

And the Easter bells chimed a solemn requiem as the flames slowly licked up the faded violets. Was it merely fancy on the wife's part, or did the husband really sigh,—a long, quivering breath of remembrance?

THREE THOUGHTS.

———

FIRST.

How few of us
In all the world's great, ceaseless strug-
   ling strife,
Go to our work with gladsome, buoyant
   step,
And love it for its sake, whate'er it be.
Because it is a labor, or, mayhap,
Some sweet, peculiar art of God's own
   gift;
And not the promise of the world's slow
   smile
Of recognition, or of mammon's gilded
   grasp.
Alas, how few, in inspiration's dazzling
   flash,
Or spiritual sense of world's beyond the
   dome
Of circling blue around this weary earth,
Can bask, and know the God-given grace
Of genius' fire that flows and permeates
The virgin mind alone; the soul in which
The love of earth hath tainted not.
The love of art and art alone.

SECOND.

"Who dares stand forth?" the monarch
    cried,
  "Amid the throng, and dare to give
  Their aid, and bid this wretch to live?
I pledge my faith and crown beside,
A woeful plight, a sorry sight,
  This outcast from all God-given grace.

  What, ho! in all, no friendly face,
No helping hand to stay his plight?
St. Peter's name be pledged for aye,
  The man's accursed, that is true;
  But ho, he suffers. None of you
Will mercy show, or pity sigh?"

Strong men drew back, and lordly train
  Did slowly file from monarch's look,
  Whose lips curled scorn. But from a
    nook
A voice cried out, "Though he has slain
That which I loved the best on earth,
  Yet will I tend him till he dies,
  I can be brave." A woman's eyes
Gazed fearlessly into his own.

THIRD.

When all the world has grown full cold
    to thee,
And man—proud pygmy—shrugs all
    scornfully,
And bitter, blinding tears flow gushing
    forth,
Because of thine own sorrows and poor
    plight,
Then turn ye swift to nature's page,
And read there passions, immeasurably
    far
Greater than thine own in all their
    littleness.
For nature has her sorrows and her joys,
As all the piled-up mountains and low
    vales
Will silently attest—and hang thy head
In dire confusion, for having dared
To moan at thine own miseries
When God and nature suffer silently.

THE WOMAN.

The literary manager of the club arose, cleared his throat, adjusted his cravat, fixed his eyes sternly upon the young man, and in a sonorous voice, a little marred by his habitual lisp, asked: " Mr. ——, will you please tell us your opinion upon the question, whether woman's chances for matrimony are increased or decreased when she becomes man's equal as a wage earner?"

The secretary adjusted her eye-glass, and held her pencil alertly poised above her book, ready to note which side Mr. —— took. Mr. —— fidgeted, pulled himself together with a violent jerk, and finally spoke his mind. Someone else did likewise, also someone else, then the women interposed, and jumped on the men, the men retaliated, a wordy war ensued, and the whole matter ended by nothing being decided, pro ·or con— generally the case in wordy discussions. *Moi?* Well, I sawed wood and said nothing, but all the while there was form-

ing in my mind, no, I won't say forming,
it was there already. It was this, *Why
should well-salaried women marry?*
Take the average working-woman of
to-day. She works from five to ten
hours a day, doing extra night work,
sometimes, of course. Her work over,
she goes home or to her boarding-house,
as the case may be. Her meals are prepared for her, she has no household
cares upon her shoulders, no troublesome
dinners to prepare for a fault-finding
husband, no fretful children to try her
patience, no petty bread and meat econ-
omies to adjust. She has her cares, her
money-troubles, her debts, and her
scrimpings, it is true, but they only make
her independent, instead of reducing her
to a dead level of despair. Her day's
work ends at the office, school, factory
or store; the rest of the time is hers,
undisturbed by the restless going to and
fro of housewifely cares, and she can em-
ploy it in mental or social diversions.
She does not incessantly rely upon the

whims of a cross man to take her to such amusements as she desires. In this nineteenth century she is free to go where she pleases — provided it be in a moral atmosphere — without comment. Theatres, concerts, lectures, and the lighter amusements of social affairs among her associates, are open to her, and there she can go, see, and be seen, admire and be admired, enjoy and be enjoyed, without a single harrowing thought of the baby's milk or the husband's coffee.

Her earnings are her own, indisputably, unreservedly, undividedly. She knows to a certainty just how much she can spend, how well she can dress, how far her earnings will go. If there is a dress, a book, a bit of music, a bunch of flowers, or a bit of furniture that she wants, she can get it, and there is no need of asking anyone's advice, or gently hinting to John that Mrs. So and So has a lovely new hat, and there is one ever so much prettier and cheaper down at Thus &

Co.'s. To an independent spirit there
is a certain sense of humiliation and
wounded pride in asking for money, be
it five cents or five hundred dollars.
The working woman knows no such
pang; she has but to question her account and all is over. In the summer
she takes her savings of the winter,
packs her trunk and takes a trip more
or less extensive, and there is none to
say her nay,—nothing to bother her
save the accumulation of her own bag-
gage. There is an independent, happy,
free-and-easy swing about the motion of
her life. Her mind is constantly being
broadened by contact with the world in its
working clothes; in her leisure moments
by the better thoughts of dead and living
men which she meets in her applications to
books and periodicals; in her vacations,
by her studies of nature, or it may be
other communities than her own. The
freedom which she enjoys she does not
trespass upon, for if she did not learn at
school she has acquired since habits of

strong self-reliance, self-support, earnest thinking, deep discriminations, and firmly believes that the most perfect liberty is that state in which humanity conforms itself to and obeys strictly, without deviation, those laws which are best fitted for their mutual self-advancement.

And so your independent working woman of to day comes as near being ideal in her equable self poise as can be imagined. So why should she hasten to give this liberty up in exchange for a serfdom, sweet sometimes, it is true, but which too often becomes galling and un-endurable.

It is not marriage that I decry, for I don't think any really sane person would do this, but it is this wholesale marrying of girls in their teens, this rushing into an unknown plane of life to avoid work. Avoid work! What housewife dares call a moment her own?

Marriages might be made in Heaven, but too often they are consummated right here on earth, based on a desire to possess the physical attractions of the woman by the man, pretty much as a child desires a toy, and an inate love of man, a wild desire not to be ridiculed by the foolish as an "old maid," and a certain delicate shrinking from the work of the world — laziness is a good name for it — by the woman. The attraction of mind to mind, the ability of one to compliment the lights and shadows in the other, the capacity of either to fulfil the duties of wife or husband — these do not enter into the contract. That is why we have divorce courts.

And so our independent woman in every year of her full, rich, well-rounded life, gaining fresh knowledge and experience, learning humanity, and particularly that portion of it which is the other gender, so well as to avoid clay-footed idols, and finally when she does consent to bear the yoke upon her shoulders, does so with perhaps less romance and glamor than her younger scoffing sisters, but with an assurance of solid and more lasting happiness. Why should she have hastened this; was aught lost by the delay?

"They say" that men don't admire this type of woman, that they prefer the soft, dainty, winning, mindless creature who cuddles into men's arms, agrees to everything they say, and looks upon them as a race of gods turned loose upon this earth for the edification of womankind. Well, may be so, but there is one thing positive, they certainly respect the independent one, and admire her, too, even if it is at a distance, and that in itself is something. As to the other part, no matter how sensible a woman is on other questions, when she falls in love she is fool enough to believe her adored one a veritable Solomon. Cuddling? Well, she may preside over conventions, brandish her umbrella at board meetings, tramp the streets soliciting subscriptions, wield the blue pencil in an editorial sanctum, hammer a type-writer, smear her nose with ink from a galley full of pied type, lead infant ideas through the tortuous mazes of c-a-t and r-a-t, plead at the bar, or wield the scalpel in a dissecting room, yet when the right moment comes, she will sink as gracefully into his manly embrace, throw her arms as lovingly around his neck, and cuddle as warmly and sweetly to his bosom as her little sister who has done nothing else but think, dream, and practice for that hour. It comes natural, you see.

TEN MINUTES' MUSING.

———

There was a terrible noise in the school-yard at intermission ; peeping out the windows the boys could be seen huddled in an immense bunch, in the middle of the yard. It looked like a fight, a mob, a knock-down,— anything, so we rushed out to the door hastily, fearfully, ready to scold, punish, console, frown, bind up broken heads or drag wounded forms from the melee as the case might be. Nearly every boy in the school was in that seething, swarming mass, and those who weren't were standing around on the edges, screaming and throwing up their hats in hilarious excitement. It was a mob, a fearful mob, but a mob apparently with a vigorous and well-defined purpose. It was a mob that screamed and howled, and kicked, and yelled, and shouted, and perspired, and squirmed, and wriggled, and pushed, and threatened, and poured itself all seemingly upon some central object. It was a mob that had an aim, that was determined to accomplish that aim, even though the whole azure expanse of sky fell upon them. It was a mob with set muscles, straining like whip-cords, eyes on that central object and with heads inward and sturdy legs outward, like prairie horses reversed in a battle. The cheerers and hat throwers on the outside were mirthful, but the mob was not; it howled, but howled without any cachinnation; it struggled for mastery. Some fell and were trampled over, some weaker ones were even tossed in the air, but the mob never deigned to trouble itself about such trivialities. It was an interesting, nervous whole, with divers parts of separate vitality.

In alarm I looked about for the principal. He was standing at a safe distance with his hands in his pockets watching the seething mass with a broad smile. At sight of my perplexed expression some one was about to venture an explanation, when there was a wild yell, a sudden vehement disintegration of the mass, a mighty rush and clutch at a dark object bobbing in the air — and the mist cleared from my intellect — as I realized it all — football.

Did you ever stop to see the analogy between a game of football and the interesting little game called life which we play every day? There is one, far-fetched as it may seem, though, for that matter, life's game, being one of desperate chances and strategic moves, is analogous to anything.

But, if we could get out of ourselves and soar above the world, far enough to view the mass beneath in its daily struggles, and near enough the hearts of the people to feel the throbs beneath their boldly carried exteriors, the whole would seem naught but such a maddening rush and senseless-looking crushing. " We are but children of a larger growth " after all, and our ceaseless pursuing after the baubles of this earth are but the struggles for precedence in the business play-ground.

The foot-ball is money. See how the mass rushes after it! Everyone so intent upon his pursuit until all else dwindles into a riduculous nonentity. The weaker ones go down in the mad pursuit, and are unmercifully trampled upon, but no matter, what is the difference if the foremost win the coveted prize and carry it off. See the big boy in front, he with iron grip, and determined, compressed lips? That boy is a type of the big, merciless man, the Gradgrind of the latter century. His face is set towards the ball, and even though he may crush a dozen small boys, he'll make his way through the mob and come out triumphant. And he'll be the victor longer than anyone else, in spite of the envy and fighting and pushing about him.

To an observer, alike unintelligent about the rules of a foot-ball game, and the conditions which govern the barter and exchange and fluctuations of the world's money market, there is as much difference between the sight of a mass of boys on a play-ground losing their equilibrium over a spheroid of rubber and a mass of men losing their coolness and temper and mental and nervous balance on change as there is between a pine sapling and a mighty forest king — merely a difference of age. The mighty, seething, intensely concentrated mass in its emphatic tendency to one point is the same, in the utter disregard of mental and physical welfare. The momentary triumphs of transitory possessions impress a casual looker-on with the same fearful idea — that the human race, after all, is savage to the core, and cultivates its savagery in an inflated happiness at its own nearness to perfection.

But the bell clangs sharply, the over-heated, nervous, tingling boys fall into line, and the sudden transition from massing disorder to military precision cuts short the ten minutes' musing.

A PLAINT.

Dear God, 'tis hard, so awful hard to lose
The one we love, and see him go afar,
With scarce one thought of aching
    hearts behind,
Nor wistful eyes, nor outstretched yearn-
    ing hands.
Chide not, dear God, if surging thoughts
    arise.
And bitter questionings of love and fate,
But rather give my weary heart thy rest,
And turn the sad, dark memories into
    sweet.
Dear God, I fain my loved one were
    anear,
But since thou will'st that happy thence
    he'll be,
I send him forth, and back I'll choke the
    grief
Rebellious rises in my lonely heart.
I pray thee, God, my loved one joy to
    bring ;
I dare not hope that joy will be with me,
But ah, dear God, one boon I crave of
    thee,
That he shall ne'er forget his hours with
    me.

IN UNCONSCIOUSNESS.

There was a big booming in my ears, great heavy iron bells that swung to-and-fro on either side, and sent out deafening reverberations that steeped the senses in a musical melody of sonorous sound; to-and-fro, backward and forward, yet ever receding in a gradually widening circle, monotonous, mournful, weird, suffusing the soul with an unutterable sadness, as images of wailing processions, of weeping, empty-armed women, and widowed maidens flashed through the mind, and settled on the soul with a crushing, o'er-pressing weight of sorrow.

Now I lay floating, arms outstretched, on an illimitable waste of calm tranquil waters. Far away as eye could reach, there was naught but the pale, white-flecked, green waters of this ocean of eternity, and above the tender blue sky arched down in perfect love of its mistress, the ocean. Sky and sea, sea and sky, blue, calm, infinite, perfect sea, heaving its womanly bosom to the passionate kisses of its ardent sun-lover. Away into infinity stretched this perfectibility of love; into eternity, I was drifting, alone, silent, yet burdened still with the remembrance of the sadness of the bells.

Far away, they tolled out the incessant dirge, grown resignedly sweet now; so intense in its infinite peace, that a calm of love, beyond all human understanding and above all earthly passions, sank deep into my soul, and so permeated my whole being with rest and peace, that my lips smiled and my eyes drooped in access of fulsome joy. Into the illimitable space of infinity we drifted, my soul and I, borne along only by the network of auburn hair that floated about me in the green waters.

———

But now, a rude grasp from somewhere is laid upon me, pressing upon my face. Instantly the air grows gloomy, gray, and the ocean rocks menacingly, while the great bells grow harsh and strident, as they hint of a dark fate. I clasp my hands appealingly to the heavens; I moan and struggle with the unknown grasp; then there is peace and the sweet content of the infinite Nirvana.

Then slowly, softly, the net of auburn hair begins to drag me down below the surface of the sea. Oh! the skies are so sweet, and now that the tender stars are looking upon us, how fair to stay and sway upon the breast of eternity! But the net is inexorable, and gently, slowly pulls me down. Now we sink straight, now we whirl in slow, eddying circles, spiral-like; while at each turn those bells ring out clanging now in wild crescendo, then whispering dread secrets of the ocean's depths. Oh, ye mighty bells, tell me from your learned lore of the hopes of mankind! Tell me what fruit he beareth from his strivings and yearn-ngs; know not ye? Why ring ye now so joyful, so hopeful; then toll your dismal prophecies of o'er-cast skies?

Years have passed, and now centuries, too, are swallowed in the gulf of eternity, yet the auburn net still whirls me in eddying circles, down, down to the very womb of time; to the innermost recesses of the mighty ocean.

———

And now, peace, perfect, unconditioned, sublime peace, and rest, and silence. For to the great depths of the mighty ocean the solemn bells cannot penetrate, and no sound, not even the beatings of one's own heart, is heard. In the heart of eternity there can be nothing to break the calm of frozen æons. In the great white hall I lay, silent, unexpectant, calm, and smiled in perfect content at the web of auburn hair which trailed across my couch. No passionate longing for life or love, no doubting question of heaven or hell, no strife for carnal needs,— only rest, content, peace — happiness, perfect, whole, complete, sublime.

And thus passed ages and ages, æons and æons. The great earth there in the dim distance above the ocean has toiled wearily about the sun, until its mechanism was failing, and the warm ardor of the lover's eye was becoming pale and cold from age, while the air all about the fast dwindling sphere was heavy and thick with the sorrows and heart-aches and woes of the humans upon its face. Heavy with the screams and roar of war; with the curses of the deceived of traitors ; with the passionate sighs of unlawful love; with the crushing unrest of blighted hopes. Knowledge and contempt of all these things permeated even to the inmost depths of time, as I lay in the halls of rest and smiled at the web floating through my white fingers.

————.

But hark! discord begins. There is a vague fear which springs from an unknown source and drifts into the depths of rest ; fear, indefinable, unaccountable, unknowable, shuddering. Pain begins, for the heart springs into life, and fills the silence with the terror of its beatings, thick, knifing, frightful in its intense longing. Power of mind over soul, power of calm over fear avail nothing; suspense and misery, locked arm in arm, pervade æonic stillness, till all things else become subordinate, unnoticed

Centuries drift away, and the giddy, old reprobate — earth, dying a hideous, ghastly death, with but one solitary human to shudder in unision with its last throes, to bask in the last pale rays of a cold sun, to inhale the last breath of a metallic atmosphere; totters, reels, falls into space, and is no more. Peal out, ye brazen bells, peal out the requiem of the sinner! Roll your mournful tones into the ears of the saddened angels, weeping with wing-covered eyes! Toll the requiem of the sinner, sinking swiftly, sobbingly into the depths of time's ocean. Down, down, until the great groans which arose from the domes and Ionic roofs about me told that the sad old earth sought rest in eternity, while the universe shrugged its shoulders over the loss of another star.

And now, the great invisible fear became apparent, tangible, for all the sins, the woes, the miseries, the dreads, the dismal achings and throbbings, the dreariness and gloom of the lost star came together and] like a huge geni took form and hideous shape — octopus-like — which slowly approached me, erstwhile happy — and hovered about my couch in fearful menace.

———

Oh, shining web of hair, burst loose your bonds and bid me move! Oh, time, cease not your calculations, but speed me on to deliverance! Oh, silence, vast, immense, infuse into your soul some sound other than the heavy throbbing of this fast disintegrating heart! Oh, pitiless stone arches, let fall your crushing weight upon this Stygian monster!

I pray to time, to eternity, to the frozen æons of the past. Useless. I am seized, forced to open my cold lips; there is agony,— supreme, mortal agony of nerve tension, and wrenching of vitality. I struggle, scream, and clutching the monster with superhuman strength, fling him aside, and rise, bleeding, screaming — but triumphant, and keenly mortal in every vein, alive and throbbing with consciousness and pain.

———

No, it was not opium, nor night-mare, but chloroform, a dentist, three obstinate molars, a pair of forceps, and a lively set of nerves.

TITEE.

It was cold that day; the great sharp north wind swept out Elysian Fields Street in blasts that made men shiver, and bent everything in its track. The skies hung lowering and gloomy; the usually quiet street was more than deserted, it was dismal.

Titee leaned against one of the brown freight cars for protection against the shrill norther, and warmed his little chapped hands at a blaze of chips and dry grass. " May be it'll snow," he muttered, casting a glance at the sky that would have done credit to a practised seaman. "Then *won't* I have fun ! Ugh, but the wind blows ! "

It was Saturday, or Titee would have been in school — the big yellow school on Marigny Street, where he went every day when its bell boomed nine o'clock. Went with a run and a joyous whoop,

— presumably to imbibe knowledge, ostensibly to make his teacher's life a burden.

Idle, lazy, dirty, troublesome boy, she called him, to herself, as day by day wore on, and Titee improved not, but let his whole class pass him on its way to a higher grade. A practical joke he relished infinitely more than a practical problem, and a good game at pinsticking was far more entertaing than a language lesson. Moreover, he was always hungry, and *would* eat in school before the half-past ten intermission, thereby losing much good play-time for his voracious appetite.

But there was nothing in natural history that Titee didn't know. He could dissect a butterfly or a mosquito-hawk and describe their parts as accurately as a spectacled student with a scalpel and microscope could talk about a cadaver. The entire Third District, with its swamps and canals and commons and rail-road sections, and its wondrous,

crooked, tortuous streets was as an open
book to Titee. There was not a nook
or corner that he did not know or could
tell of. There was not a bit of gossip
among the gamins, little Creole and
Spanish fellows, with dark skins and
lovely eyes like Spaniels, that Titee could
not tell of. He knew just exactly when
it was time for crawfish to be plentiful
down in the Claiborne and Marigny
canals; just when a poor, breadless fellow might get a job in the big bone-
yard and fertilizing factory out on the
railroad track; and as for the levee, with
its ships and schooners and sailors —
Oh, how he could revel among them!
The wondrous ships, the pretty little
schooners, where the foreign-looking
sailors lay on long moon-lit nights, singing gay bar carols to the tinkle of a
guitar and mandolin. All these things,
and more, could Titee tell of. He had
been down to the Gulf, and out on its
treacherous waters through Eads Jetties
on a fishing smack, with some jolly,

brown sailors, and could interest the whole school-room in the "talk lessons," if he chose.

Titee shivered as the wind swept round the freight cars. There isn't much warmth in a bit of a jersey coat.

"Wish 'twas summer," he murmured, casting another sailor's glance at the sky. "Don't believe I like snow, it's too wet and cold." And, with a last parting caress at the little fire he had builded for a minute's warmth, he plunged his hands in his pockets, shut his teeth, and started manfully on his mission out the railroad track towards the swamps.

It was late when Titee came home, to such a home as it was, and he had but illy performed his errand, so his mother beat him, and sent him to bed supperless. A sharp strap stings in cold weather, and long walks in the teeth of a biting wind creates a keen appetite. But if Titee cried himself to sleep that night, he was up bright and early next morning, and had been to early mass, devoutly kneeling on the cold floor, blowing his fingers to keep them warm, and was home almost before the rest of the family was awake.

There was evidently some great matter of business in this young man's mind, for he scarcely ate his breakfast, and had left the table, eagerly cramming the remainder of his meal in his pockets.

"I wonder what he's up to now?" mused his mother as she watched his little form sturdily trudging the track in the face of the wind, his head, with the rimless cap thrust close on the shock of black hair, bent low, his hands thrust deep in the bulging pockets.

"A new snake, perhaps," ventured the father ; "he's a queer child."

But the next day Titee was late for school. It was something unusual, for he was always the first on hand to fix some plan of mechanism to make the teacher miserable. She looked reprovingly at him this morning, when he came in during the arithmetic class, his hair all wind-blown, cheeks rosy from a hard fight with the sharp blasts. But he made up for his tardiness by his extreme goodness all day ; just think, Titee didn't even eat in school. A something unparalleled in the entire history of his school-life.

When the lunch-hour came, and all the yard was a scene of feast and fun, one of the boys found him standing by one of the posts, disconsolately watching a ham sandwich as it rapidly disappeared down the throat of a sturdy, square-headed little fellow.

" Hello, Edgar," he said, " What yer got fer lunch? "

" Nothin ', " was the mournful reply.

" Ah, why don't yer stop eatin' in school fer a change ? Yer don't ever have nothin' to eat."

" I didn't eat to-day," said Titee, blazing up.

" Yer did! "

" I tell you I didn't! " and Titee's hard little fist planted a punctuation mark on his comrade's eye.

A fight in the school-yard! Poor Titee in disgrace again. But in spite of his battered appearance, a severe scolding from the principal, lines to write, and a further punishment from his mother, Titee scarcely remained for his dinner, but was off, down the railroad track, with his pockets partly stuffed with the remnants of his scanty meal.

And the next day Titee was tardy again, and lunchless, too, and the next, and the next, until the teacher in despair sent a nicely printed note to his mother about him, which might have done some good, had not Titee taken great pains to tear it up on his way home.

But one day it rained, whole bucketfuls of water, that poured in torrents from a miserable angry sky. Too wet a day for bits of boys to be trudging to school, so Titee's mother thought, so kept him home to watch the weather through the window, fretting and fuming, like a regular storm-cloud in miniature. As the day wore on, and the storm did not abate, his mother had to keep a strong watch upon him, or he would have slipped away.

At last dinner came and went, and the gray soddenness of the skies deepened into the blackness of coming night. Someone called Titee to go to bed—and Titee was nowhere to be found.

Under the beds, in corners and closets, through the yard, and in such impossible places as the soap-dish and the water-pitcher even; but he had gone as completely as if he had been spirited away. It was of no use to call up the neighbors; he had never been near their houses, they affirmed, so there was nothing to do but to go to the rail-road track, where little Titee had been seen so often trudging in the shrill north wind.

So with lantern and sticks, and his little yellow dog, the rescuing party started out the track. The rain had ceased falling, but the wind blew a tremendous gale, scurrying great, gray clouds over a fierce sky. It was not exactly dark, though in this part of the city, there was neither gas nor electricity, and surely on such a night as this, neither moon nor stars dared show their faces in such a grayness of sky; but a sort of all-diffused luminosity was in the air, as though the sea of atmosphere was charged with an ethereal phosphorescence.

Search as they would, there were no signs of poor little Titee. The soft earth between the railroad ties crumbled beneath their feet without showing any small tracks or foot-prints.

"Let us return," said the big brother, "he can't be here anyway."

"No, no," urged the mother, "I feel that he is; let's go on."

So on they went, slipping on the wet earth, stumbling over the loose rocks, until a sudden wild yelp from Tiger brought them to a standstill. He had rushed ahead of them, and his voice could be heard in the distance, howling piteously.

With a fresh impetus the little muddy party hurried forward. Tiger's yelps could be heard plainer and plainer, mingled now with a muffled wail, as of some one in pain.

And then, after awhile they found a pitiful little heap of wet and sodden rags, lying at the foot of a mound of earth and stones thrown upon the side of the track. It was little Titee with a broken leg, all wet and miserable, and moaning.

They picked him up tenderly, and started to carry him home. But he cried and clung to his mother, and begged not to go.

" He's got fever," wailed his mother.

" No , no, it's my old man. He's hungry, sobbed Titee, holding out a little package. It was the remnants of his dinner, wet and rain washed.

" What old man ?" asked the big brother.

" My old man, oh, please, please don't go home until I see him, I'm not hurting much, I can go."

So yielding to his whim, they carried him further away, down the sides of the track up to an embankment or levee by the sides of the Marigny canal. Then Titee's brother, suddenly stopping, exclaimed :

"Why, here's a cave, a regular Robinson Cruso affair."

"It's my old man's cave," cried Titee ; "oh, please go in, maybe he's dead."

There can't be much ceremony in entering a cave, there is but one thing to do, walk in. This they did, and holding high the lantern, beheld a strange sight. On a bed of straw and paper in one corner lay a withered, wizened, white-bearded old man, with wide eyes staring at the unaccustomed sight. In the corner lay a cow.

"It's my old man!" cried Titee, joyfully. "Oh, please, grandpa, I couldn't get here to-day, it rained all morning, and when I ran away this evening, I slipped down and broke something, and oh, grandpa, I'm so tired and hurty, and

I'm so afraid you're hungry."

So the secret of Titee's jaunts out the railroad was out. In one of his trips around the swamp-land, he had discovered the old man dying from cold and hunger in the fields. Together they had found this cave, and Titee had gathered the straw and brush that scattered itself over the ground and made the bed. A poor old cow turned adrift by an ungrateful master, had crept in and shared the damp dwelling. And thither Titee had trudged twice a day, carrying his luncheon in the morning, and his dinner in the evening, the sole support of a half-dead cripple.

" There's a crown in Heaven for that child," said the officer to whom the case was referred.

And so there was, for we scattered winter roses on his little grave down in old St. Rocque's cemetery. The cold and rain, and the broken leg had told their tale.

ANARCHY ALLEY.

To the casual observer, the quaint, narrow, little alley that lies in the heart of the city is no more than any other of the numerous divisions of steets in which New Orleans delights. But to the idle wanderer, or he whose mission down its four squares of much trodden stones, is an aimless one,— whose eyes unforced to bend to the ground in thought of sordid ways and means, can peer at will into its quaint corners. Exchange Alley presents all the phases of a Latinized portion of America, a bit of Europe, perhaps, the restless, chafing; anarchistic Europe of to-day, in the midst of the quieter democratic institution of our republic.

It is Bohemia, pure and simple, Bohemia, in all its stages, from the beer saloon and the cheap book-store, to the cheaper cook shop and uncertain lodging house. There the great American institution, the wondrous monarch whom the country supports — the tramp — basks in superior comfort and contented, unmolested indolence. Idleness and labor, poverty and opulence, the honest, law-abiding workingman, and the reckless, restless anarchist, jostle side by side, and brush each other's elbows in terms of equality as they do nowhere else.

On the busiest thoroughfares in the city, just in the busiest part, between two of the most crowded and conservative of cross-streets, lies this alley of Latinism. One might almost pass it hurriedly, avoiding the crowds that cluster at this section of the streets, but upon turning into a narrow section, stone-paved, the place is entered, appearing to end one square distant, seeming to bar itself from the larger buildings by an aimless sort of iron affair, part railing, part posts. There is a conservative book-store at the entrance on one side, and an even more harmless clothing

store on the other ; then comes a saloon
with many blind doors, behind which are
vistas of tables, crowded and crowded
with men drinking beer out of " globes,"
large, round, moony, common affairs.
There is a dingy, pension-claim office,
with cripples and sorrowful-looking women in black, sitting about on rickety
chairs. Somehow, there is always an
impression with me that the mourning
dress and mournful looks are put on to
impress the dispenser and adjuster. It
is wicked, but what can one do if im-
pressions come ?

There are more little cuddies of places,
dye-shops, tailors, and nondescript corners that seem to have no possible mission on earth and are sadly conscious
of their aimlessness. Then the railing
is reached, and the alley instead of ending has merely given itself an angular
twist to the right, and extends three
squares further, to a great, pale green
dome, and stately entrance.

The calmly-thinking, quietly-laboring,
cool and conservative world is for the
nonce left behind. With the first step-

ping across Customhouse street, the place widens architecturally, and the atmosphere, too, seems impregnated with a sort of mental freedom, conducive to dangerous theorizing and broody reflections on the inequality of the classes. The sun shines in a strip in the centre, yellow and elusive, like gold ; someone is rattling a gay galop on a piano somewhere ; there is a sound of mens' voices in a heated discussion, a long whiff of pipe-smoke trails through the sunlight from the bar-room ; the clink of glasses, the chink of silver, and the high treble of a woman's voice scolding a refractory child, mingle in incongruous melody.

Two-story houses all along ; the first floor divided into cuddies, here a paper store, displaying ten-cent novels of detective stories with impossible cuts, illustrating impossible situations of the plot ; dye-shops, jewelers, tailors, tin-smiths, cook-shops, intelligence offices—many of these, and some newspaper offices. On the second floor, balconies, dingy, iron-railed, with sickly box-plants, and decrepid garments airing and being turned and tended by dishevelled, slipshod women. Lodging-houses these, some of them, but one is forced to wonder why do the tenants sun their clothes so often? The lines stretched from posts to posts seem always filled with airing garments. Is it economy? And do the owners of the faded vests and patched coats hide in dusky corners while their only garments are receiving the benefit of Old Sol's cleansing rays? And are the women with the indiscriminate tresses, near relatives, or only the landladies? It would be something worth knowing if one could.

Plenty of saloons—great, gorgeous, gaudy places, with pianos and swift-footed waiters, tables and cards, and men, men, men. The famous Three Brothers' Saloon occupies a position about midway the alley, and at its doors, the acme, the culminating point, the superlative degree of unquietude and discontent is reached. It is the headquarters of nearly all the great labor organizations in the city. Behind its doors, swinging as easily between the street and the liquor-fumed halls as the soul swings between right and wrong, the disturbed minds of the working-men become clouded, heated, and wrothily ready for deeds of violence.

Outside on the pavements with hundreds of like-excited men, with angry discussions and bitter recitals of complaints, the seeds of discord sown some time since, perhaps, sprout afresh, blossom and bear fruits. Is there a strike? Then special minions of the law are detailed to this place, for violence and hatred of employers, insurrection and socialism find here ready followers. Impromptu mass meetings are common, and law-breaking schemes find their cradle beneath its glittering lights. It is always thronged within and without, a veritable nursery of riot and disorder.

And oh, Bohemia, pipes, indolence and beer! The atmosphere is impregnated with it, the dust sifts it into your clothes and hair, the sunlight filters it through your brain, the stray snatches of music now and then beat it rhythmically into your mind. There are some who work, yes, and a few places outside of the saloons that seem to be animated with a business motive. There are even some who push their way briskly through the aimless bodies of men,—but then there must be an occa-

sional anomaly to break the monotony,
If nothing more.

It is so unlike the ordinary world, this
bit of Bohemia, that one feels a personal
grievance when the marble entrance
and great, green dome become positive,
solid, architectural facts, standing in all
the grim solemnity of the main entrance
of the Hotel Royal on St. Louis Street,
ending, with a sudden return to aristoc-
racy, this stamping ground for anarchy.

IMPRESSIONS.

THOUGHT.

A swift, successive chain of things,
  That flash, kaleidoscope-like, now in,
    now out,
Now straight, now eddying in wild rings,
  No order, neither law, compels their
    moves,
  But endless, constant, always swiftly
    roves.

HOPE.

Wild seas of tossing, writhing waves,
A wreck half-sinking in the tortuous
    gloom ;
One man clings desperately, while Boreas
    raves,
  And helps to blot the rays of moon
    and star,
  Then comes a sudden flash of light,
    which gleams on shores afar.

LOVE.

A bed of roses, pleasing to the eye,

Flowers of heaven, passionate and
pure,
Upon this bed the youthful often lie,
And pressing hard upon its sweet
delight,
The cruel thorns pierce soul and heart,
and cause a woeful blight.

DEATH.

A traveller who has always heard
That on this journey he some day must
go,
Yet shudders now, when at the fatal
word
He starts upon the lonesome, dreary
way,
The past, a page of joy and woe,—
the future, none can say.

FAITH.

Blind clinging to a stern, stone cross,
Or it may be of frailer make ;
Eyes shut, ears closed to earth's drear
dross,
Immovable, serene, the world away
From thoughts — the mind uncaring
for another day.

SALAMMBO.

BY GUSTAVE FLAUBERT.

————

Like unto the barbaric splendor, the clashing of arms, the flashing of jewels, so is this book, full of brightness that dazzles, yet does not weary, of rich mosaic beauty of sensuous softness. Yet, with it all, there is a singular lack of elevation of thought and expression; everything tends to degrade, to drag the mind to a worse than earthly level. The crudity of the warriors, the minute description of the battles, the leper, Hann; even the sensual love-scene of Salammbo and Matho, and the rites of Taint and Moloch. Possibly this is due to the peculiar shortness and crispness of the sentences, and the painstaking attention to details. Nothing is left for the imagination to complete. The slightest turn of the hand, the smallest bit of tapestry and armor,—all, all is described until one's brain becomes weary with the scintillating flash of minutia. Such careful attention wearies and disappoints, and sometimes, instead of photographing the scenes indelibly upon the mental vision, there ensues only a confused mass of armor and soldiers, plains and horses.

But the description of action and movement are incomparable, resembling somewhat, in the rush and flow of words, the style of Victor Hugo; the breathless rush and fire, the restrained passion and fury of a master-hand.

Throughout the whole book this peculiarity is noticeable — there are no dissertations, no pauses for the author to express his opinions, no stoppages to reflect,—we are rushed onward with almost breathless haste, and many times are fain to pause and re-read a sentence, a paragraph, sometimes a whole page. Like the unceasing motion of a column of artillery in battle, like the roar and fury of the Carthaginian's elephant, so is the torrent of Flanbert's eloquence — majestic, grand, intense, with nobility, sensuous, but never sublime, never elevating, never delicate.

As an historian, Flanbert would have ranked high—at least in impartiality. Not once in the whole volume does he allow his prejudices, his opinions, his sentiments to crop out. We lose complete sight of the author in his work. With marvellous fidelity he explains the movements, the vices and the virtues of each party, and with Shakespearean tact, he conceals his identity, so that we are troubled with none of that Byronic vice of ' dipping one's pen into one's self.'

Still, for all the historian's impartiality, he is just a trifle incorrect, here and there —the ancients mention no aqueduct in or near Carthage. Hann was not crucified outside of Tunis. The incident of the Carthaginian women cutting off their tresses to furnish strings for bows and catapults is generally conceded to have occurred during the latter portion of the third Punic War. And still another difficulty presents itself— Salammbo was supposed to have been the only daughter of Hamilcar; according to Flanbert she dies unmarried, or rather on her wedding day, and yet historians tell us that after the death of the elder Barca, Hannibal was brought up and watched over by Hamilcar's son-in-law, Hasdrubal. Can it be possible that the crafty Numidian King, Nari Havas, is the intrepid, fearless and whole-souled Hasdrubal? Or is it only another deviation from the beaten track of history? In a historical novel, however, and one so evidently arranged for dramatic effects, such lapses from the truth only heighten the interest and kindle the imagination to a brighter flame.

The school of realism of which Zola, Tolstoi, De Maupassant, and others of that ilk are followers, claims its descent from the author of Salammbo. Perhaps their claim is well-founded, perhaps not; we are inclined to believe that it is, for every page in this novel is crowded with details, often disgusting, which are generally left out in ordinary works. The hideous deformity, the rottenness and repulsiveness of the leper Hann is brought out in such vivid detail that we sicken and fain would turn aside in disgust. But go where one will, the ghastly, quivering, wretched picture is always before us in all its filth and splendid misery. The reeking horrors of the battle-fields, the disgusting details of the army imprisoned in the defile of the battle-axe, the grimness of the sacrifices to the blood-thirsty god, Moloch, the wretchedness of Hamilcar's slaves are presented with every ghastly detail, with every degrading trick of expression. Picture after picture of misery and foulness arises and pursues us as the grim witches pursued the hapless Tam O'Shanter, clutching us in ghastly arms, clinging to us with grim and ghoulish tenacity.

Viewing the character through the

genteel crystal of nineteenth century
civilization, they are all barbarous, unnatural, intensified ; but considering the
age in which they lived— the tendencies
of that age, the gods they worshipped,
the practices in which they indulged,—
they are all true to life, perfect in the de-
piction of their natures. Spendius is a
true Greek, crafty, lying, deceitful, ungrateful. Hamilcar needs no novelist
to crystalize his character in words, he
always remains the same Hamilcar of
history, so it is with Hann ; but to Flanbert alone are we indebted for the
hideous realism of his external aspect.
Matho is a dusky son of Libya,—fierce,
passionate, resentful, unbridled in his
speech and action, swept by the hot
breath of furious love as his native sands
are swept by the burning simoon. Salammbo, cold and strange delving deep
in the mysticism of the Carthaginian
gods, living apart from human passions
in her intense love for the goddess, Tanit ;
Salammbo, in the earnest excess of her

religious fervor, eagerly accepting the mission given her by the puzzled Sarach-arabim; Salammbo, twining the gloomy folds of the python about her perfumed limbs; Salammbo, resisting, then yielding to the fierce love of Matho; Salammbo, dying when her erstwhile lover expires; Salammbo, in all her many phases reminds us of some early Christian martyr or saint, though the sweet spirit of the Great Teacher is hidden in the punctual devotion to the mysterious rites of Tanit. She is an inexplicable mixture of the tropical exotic and the frigid snow-flower,— a rich and rare growth that attracts and repulses, that interests and absorbs, that we admire — without loving, detest — without hating.

LEGEND OF THE NEWSPAPER.

Poets sing and fables tell us,
Or old folk lore whispers low,
Of the origin of all things,
Of the spring from whence they came,
Kalevala, old and hoary,
Æneid, Iliad, Æsop, too,
All are filled with strange quaint legends,
All replete with ancient tales,—

How love came, and how old earth,
Freed from chaos, grew for us,
To a green and wondrous spheroid,
To a home for things alive;
How fierce fire and iron cold,
How the snow and how the frost,—
All these things the old rhymes ring,
All these things the old tales tell.

Yet they ne'er sang of the beginning,
Of that great unbreathing angel,
Of that soul without a haven,
Of that gracious Lady Bountiful,
Yet they ne'er told how it came here;
Ne'er said why we read it daily,

Nor did they even let us guess why
We were left to tell the tale.

Came one day into the wood-land,
Muckintosh, the great and mighty,
Muckintosh, the famous thinker,
He whose brain was all his weapons,
As against his rival's soarings,
High unto the vaulted heavens,
Low adown the swarded earth,
Rolled he round his gaze all steely,
And his voice like music prayed :
"Oh, Creator, wondrous Spirit,
Thou who hast for us descended
In the guise of knowledge mighty,
And our brains with truth o'er-flooded ;
In the greatness of thy wisdom,
Knowest not our limitations?
Wondrous thoughts have we, thy ser-
        vants,
Wondrous things we see each day,
Yet we cannot tell our brethren,
Yet we cannot let them know,
Of our doings and our happenings,
Should they parted be from us?
Help us, oh, Thou Wise Creator,

From the fulness of thy wisdom,
Show us how to spread our knowledge,
And disseminate our actions,
Such as we find worthy, truly.

Quick the answer came from heaven ;
Muckintosh, the famous thinker,
Muckintosh, the great and mighty,
Felt a trembling, felt a quaking,
Saw the earth about him open,
Saw the iron from the mountains
Form a quaint and queer machine,
Saw the lead from out the lead mines
Roll into small lettered forms,
Saw the fibres from the flax-plant,
Spread into great sheets of paper,
Saw the ink galls from the green trees
Crushed upon the leaden forms ;
Muckintosh, the famous thinker,
Muckintosh, the great and mighty,
Felt a trembling, felt a quaking,
Saw the earth about him open,
Saw the flame and sulphur smoking,
Came the printer's little devil,
Far from distant lands the printer,
Man of unions, man of cuss-words,

From the depths of sooty blackne ss ;
Came the towel of the printer ;
Many things that Muckintosh saw,—
Galleys, type, and leads and rules,
Presses, press-men, quoins and spaces,
Quads and caps and lower cases.

But to Muckintosh bewildered,
All this passed as in a dream,
Till within his nervous hand,
Hand with joy and fear a-quaking,
Muckintosh, the great and mighty,
Muckintosh, the famous thinker,
Held the first of our newspapers.

A CARNIVAL JANGLE.

There is a merry jangle of bells in the air, an all-pervading sense of jester's noise, and the flaunting vividness of royal colors; the streets swarm with humanity,— humanity in all shapes, manners, forms,— laughing, pushing, jostling, crowding, a mass of men and women and children, as varied and as assorted in their several individual peculiarities as ever a crowd that gathered in one locality since the days of Babel.

It is Carnival in New Orleans; a brilliant Tuesday in February, when the very air effervesces an ozone intensely exhilirating—of a nature half spring, half winter—to make one long to cut capers. The buildings are a blazing mass of royal purple and golden yellow, and national flags, bunting and decorations that laugh in the glint of the Midas sun. The streets a crush of jesters and maskers, Jim Crows and clowns, ballet girls and Mephistos, Indians and monkeys; of wild and sudden flashes of music, of glittering pageants and comic ones, of befeathered and belled horses. A madding dream of color and melody and fantasy gone wild in an effervescent bubble of beauty that shifts and changes and passes kaleidoscope-like before the bewildered eye.

A bevy of bright-eyed girls and boys of that uncertainty of age that hovers between childhood and maturity, were moving down Canal Street when there was a sudden jostle with another crowd meeting them. For a minute there was a deafening clamor of laughter, cracking of whips, which all maskers carry, jingle and clatter of carnival bells, and the masked and unmasked extricated themselves and moved from each other's paths. But in the confusion a tall Prince of Darkness had whispered to one of the girls in the unmasked crowd: " You'd better come with us, Flo, you're wasting time in that tame gang. Slip off, they'll never miss you ; we'll get you a rig, and show you what life is."

And so it happened that when a half hour passed, and the bright-eyed bevy missed Flo and couldn't find her, wisely giving up the search at last, that she, the quietest and most bashful of the lot, was being initiated into the mysteries of " what life is."

Down Bourbon Street and on Toulouse and St. Peter Streets there are quaint little old-world places, where one may be disguised effectually for a tiny consideration. Thither guided by the shapely Mephisto, and guarded by the team of jockeys and ballet girls, tripped Flo. Into one of the lowest-ceiled, dingiest and most ancient-looking of these disguise shops they stopped.

"A disguise for this demoiselle," announced Mephisto to the woman who met them. She was small and wizened and old, with yellow, flabby jaws and neck like the throat of an alligator, and straight, white hair that stood from her head uncannily stiff.

" But the demoiselle wishes to appear a boy, *un petit garçon* ? " she inquired, gazing eagerly at Flo's long, slender frame. Her voice was old and thin, like the high quavering of an imperfect tuning fork, and her eyes were sharp as talons in their grasping glance.

" Mademoiselle does not wish such a costume," gruffly responded Mephisto.

" *Ma foi*, there is no other," said the ancient, shrugging her shoulders. " But one is left now, mademoiselle would make a fine troubadour."

" Flo," said Mephisto, " it's a dare-devil scheme, try it ; no one will ever know it but us, and we'll die before we tell. Besides, we must ; it's late, and you couldn't find your crowd."

And that was why you might have seen a Mephisto and a slender troubadour of lovely form, with mandolin flung across his shoulder, followed by a bevy of jockeys and ballet girls, laughing and singing as they swept down Rampart Street.

When the flash and glare and brilliancy of Canal Street have palled upon the tired eye, and it is yet too soon to go home, and to such a prosaic thing as dinner, and one still wishes for novelty, then it is wise to go in the lower districts. Fantasy and fancy and grotesqueness in the costuming and behavior of the maskers run wild. Such dances and whoops and leaps as these hideous Indians and devils do indulge in; such wild curvetings and great walks. And in the open squares, where whole groups do congregate, it is wonderfully amusing. Then, too, there is a ball in every available hall, a delirious ball, where one may dance all day for ten cents; dance and grow mad for joy, and never know who were your companions, and be yourself unknown. And in the exhiliration of the day, one walks miles and miles, and dances and curvets, and the fatigue is never felt.

In Washington Square, away down where Royal Street empties its stream

of children and men into the broad channel of Elysian Fields Avenue, there was
a perfect Indian dance. With a little
imagination one might have willed away
the vision of the surrounding houses and
fancied one's self again in the forest,
where the natives were holding a sacred
riot. The square was filled with spectators, masked and unmasked. It was
amusing to watch these mimic Red-men,
they seemed so fierce and earnest.

Suddenly one chief touched another
on the elbow. "See that Mephisto and
troubadour over there?" he whispered
huskily.

"Yes, who are they?"

"I don't know the devil," responded
the other quietly, "but I'd know that
other form anywhere. It's Leon, see?
I know those white hands like a woman's
and that restless head. Ha!

"But there may be a mistake."

"No. I'd know that one anywhere;
I feel it's him. I'll pay him now. Ah,
sweetheart, you've waited long, but you

shall feast now !" He was caressing
something long, and lithe, and glittering
beneath his blanket.

In a masked dance it is easy to give a
death-blow between the shoulders. Two
crowds meet and laugh and shout and
mingle almost inextricably, and if a
shriek of pain should arise, it is not
noticed in the din, and when they part,
if one should stagger and fall bleeding
to the ground, who can tell who has
given the blow ? There is naught but
an unknown stiletto on the ground, the
crowd has dispersed, and masks tell no
tales anyway. There is murder, but by
whom ? for what ? *Quien sabe ?*

And that is how it happened on Carnival night, in the last mad moments of
Rex's reign, a broken-hearted woman
sat gazing wide-eyed and mute at a
horrible something that lay across the
bed. Outside the long sweet march
music of many bands floated in in
mockery, and the flash of rockets and
Bengal lights illumined the dead, white
face of the girl troubadour.

PAUL TO VIRGINIA.

FIN DE SIECLE.

I really must confess, my dear,
   I cannot help but love you,
For of all girls I ever knew,
   There's none I place above you ;
But then you know it's rather hard,
   To dangle aimless at your skirt,
And watch your every movement so,
   For I am jealous, and you're a flirt.

There's half a score of fellows round,
   You smile at every one,
And as I think to pride myself for bask-
      ing in the sun
Of your sweet smiles, you laugh at me,
   And treat me like a lump of dirt,
Until I wish that I were dead,
   For I am jealous, and you're a flirt.

I'm sorry that I've ever known
   Your loveliness entrancing,
Or ever saw your laughing eyes,
   With girlish mischief dancing;
'Tis agony supreme and rare

To see your slender waist a-girt
With other fellows' arms, you see,
For I am jealous, and you're a flirt.
Now, girlie, if you'll promise me,
To never, never treat me mean,
I'll show you in a little while,
The best sweetheart you've ever seen ;
You do not seem to know or care,
How often you've my feelings hurt,
While flying round with other boys,
For I am jealous, and you're a flirt.

THE MAIDEN'S DREAM.

The maid had been reading love-poetry, where the world lay bathed in moon-light, fragrant with dew-wet roses and jasmine, harmonious with the clear tinkle of mandolin and guitar. Then a lethargy, like unto that which steeps the senses, and benumbs the faculties of the lotus-eaters, enveloped her brain, and she lay as one in a trance,— awake, yet sleeping; conscious, yet unburdened with care.

And there stole into her consciousness, words, thoughts, not of her own, yet she read them not, nor heard them spoken; they fell deep into her heart and soul, softer and more caressing than the over-shadowing wing of a mother-dove, sweeter and more thrilling than the last high notes of a violin, and they were these:—

Love, most potent, most tyrannical, and most gentle of the passions which

sway the human mind, thou art the invisible agency which rules mens' souls,
which governs mens' kingdoms, which
controls the universe. By thy mighty
will do the silent, eternal hosts of Heaven
sweep in sublime procession across the
unmeasured blue. The perfect harmony
of the spheres is attuned for thee, and
by thee; the perfect coloring of the
clouds, than which no mortal pigment
can dare equal, are thy handiwork.
Most ancient of the heathen deities,
Eros; powerful God of the Christians,
Jehovah, all hail ! For a brief possession
of thy divine fire have kingdoms waxed
and waned; men in all the bitterness of
hatred fought, bled, died by millions,
their grosser selves to be swept into the
bosom of their ancient mother, an immense holocaust to thee. For thee and
thee alone does the world prosper; for
thee do men strive to become better
than their fellow-men; for thee, and
through thee have they sunk to such
depths of degradation as causes a blush

to be painted upon the faces of those that see. All things are subservient to thee. All the delicate intricate workings of that marvellous machine, the human brain ; all the passions and desires of the human heart,— ambition, desire, greed, hatred, envy, jealousy, all others. Thou breedst them all, O love, thou art all-potent, all-wise, infinite, eternal ! Thy power is felt by mortals in all ages, all climes, all conditions. Behold !

A picture came into the maiden's eye : a broad and fertile plain, tender verdure, soft blue sky overhead, with white billowy clouds nearing the horizon like great airy, snow-capped mountains. The soft warm breeze from the south whispered faintly through the tall, slender palms and sent a thrill of joy through the frisky lambkins, who capered by the sides of their graver dams. And there among the riches of the flock stood Laban, haughty, stern, yet withal a kindly gleam in the glance which rested upon the group about him. Hoary the beard that rested upon his breast, but steady the hand that stretched in blessing. Leah, the tender-eyed, the slighted, is there; and Rachel, young and beautiful and blushing beneath the ardent gaze of her handsome lover. "And Jacob loved Rachel, and said, I will serve thee seven years for Rachel, thy younger daughter."

How different the next scene! Heaven's wrath burst loose upon a single community. Fire, the red-winged demon with brazen throat wide opened, hangs his brooding wings upon an erstwhile happy city. Hades has climbed through the crater of Vesuvius, and leaps in fiendish waves along the land. Few the souls escaping, and God have mercy upon those who stumble through the blinding darkness, made more torturingly hideous by the intermittent flashes of lurid light. And yet there come three, whom the darkness seems not to deter, nor obstacles impede. Only a blind person, accustomed to constant darkness, and familiarized with these streets could walk that way. Nearer they come, a burst of flames thrown into the inky firmament by impish hands, reveals Glaucus, supporting the half-fainting Ione, following Nydia, frail, blind, flower-loving Nydia, sacrificing life for her unloving beloved.

And then the burning southern sun shone bright and golden o'er the silken sails of the Nile serpent's ships; glinted on the armor and weapons of the famous galley; shone with a warm caressing touch upon her beauty, as though it loved this queen, as powerful in her sphere as he in his. It is at Actium, and the fate of nations and generations yet unborn hang, as the sword of Damocles hung, upon the tiny thread of destiny. Egypt herself, her splendid barbaric beauty acting like an inspiration upon the craven followers, leads on, foremost in this fierce struggle. Then, the tide turns, and overpowered, they fly before disgrace and defeat. Antony is

there, the traitor, dishonored, false to
his country, yet true to his love; Antony, whom ambition could not lure
from her passionate caresses; Antony,
murmuring softly,—

Egypt, thou knowest too well
My heart was to thy rudder tied by the
    strings,
And thou should'st tow me after.
Over my spirit
Thy full supremacy thou knewest,
And that thy beck might from the bid-
    ding of the gods
Command me.

Picture after picture flashed through
the maiden's mind. Agnes, the gentle,
sacrificing, burrowing like some frantic
animal through the ruins of Lisbon,
saving her lover, Franklin, by teeth and
bleeding hands. Dora, the patient,
serving a loveless existence, saving her
rival from starvation and destitution.
The stern, dark, exiled Florentine poet,
with that one silver ray in his clouded
life — Beatrice.

She heard the piping of an elfish voice, "Mother, why does the minister keep his hands over his heart?" and the white drawn face of Hester Prynne, with her scarlet elf-child, passed slowly across her vision. The wretched misery of deluded Lucius and his mysterious Lamia she saw, and watched with breathless interest the formation of that "Brotherhood of the Rose." There was radiant Armorel, from sea-blown, wave-washed Lyonesse, her perfect head poised in loving caress over the magic violin. Dark-eyed Corinne, head drooped gently as she improvised those Rome-famed world symphonies passed, almost ere Edna and St. Elmo had crossed the threshold of the church happy in the love now consecrated through her to God. Oh, the pictures, the forms, the love-words which crowded her mind! They thrilled her heart, crushed out all else save a crushing, over-powering sense of perfect, complete joy. A joy that sought to express

itself in wondrous melodies and silences,
filled with thoughts too deep and sacred
for words.　Overpowered with the magnificence of his reign, overwhelmed with
the complete subjugation of all things
unto him, do you wonder that she awoke
and placing both hands into those of
the lover at her side, whispered : —
Take all of me — I am thine own, heart,
　　soul,
　Brain, body, all; all that I am or
　　dream
Is thine forever? yea, though space
　　should teem
With thy conditions, I'd fulfil the whole,
Were to fulfil them to be loved by thee.

IN MEMORIAM.

The light streams through the windows
    arched high,
    And o'er the stern, stone carvings
      breaks
    In warm rich gold and crimson waves,
Then steals away in corners dark to die.

And all the grand cathedral silence falls
    Into the hearts of those that worship
      low,
    Like tender waves of hushed nothing-
      ness,
Confined nor kept by human earthly
    walls.

Deep music in its thundering organ
    sounds,
    Grows diffuse through the echoing
      space,
    Till hearts grow still in sadness'
      mighty joy,
Or leap aloft in swift ecstatic bounds.

Mayhap 'twas but a dream that came to
    me,
    Or but a vision of the soul's desire,
    To see the nation in one mighty
    whole,
Do homage on its bended, worshipping
    knee.

Through time's heroic actions, the soul
    of man,
    Alone proves what that soul without
    earth's dross
    Could be, and this, through time's
    far-searching fire,
Hath proved thine white beneath the
    deepest scan.

A woman's tribute, 'tis a tiny dot,
    A merest flower from a frail, small
    hand,
    To lay among the many petaled
    wreaths
About thy form,— a tribute soon forgot.

But if in all the incense to arise
    In fragrance to the blue empyrean

The blended sweetness of the womens'
   love
Goes pouring too, in all their heartfelt
   sighs,

And if one woman's sorrow be among
   them too,
  One woman's joy for labor past
  Be reckoned in the mighty teeming
   whole,
It is enough, there is not more to do.

Within the hearts of heroes small an d
   great
  There 'bides a tenderness for weakling things
   Within thy heart, the sorrowing
   country knows
The se passions, bravest and the tender-
   est mate.

When man is dust, before the gazing
   eyes
  Of all the gaping throng, his life lies
   wide
  For all to see and whisper low about

Or let their thoughts in discord's clatter
   rise.

But thine was pure and undefiled,
   A record of long brilliant, teeming
      days,
   Each thought did tend to further
      things,
But pure as the proverbial child.

Oh, people, that thy grief might find ex-
      press
   To gather in some vast cathedral's
      hall,
   That then in unity we might kneel
      and hear
Sublimity in sounds, voice our distress.

Peace, peace, the men of God cry, ye be
      bold,
   The world hath known, 'tis Heaven
      who claims him now,
   And in our railings we but cast aside
The noble traits he bid us hold.
So though divided through the land, in
      dreams
   We see a people kneeling low,

Bowed down in heart and soul to see
This fearful sorrow, crushing as it seems.
And all the grand cathedral silence falls
 Into the hearts of these that worship
  low,
 Like tender waves of hushed nothing-
  ness,
Confined, nor kept by human earthly
 walls.

A STORY OF VENGEANCE.

Yes, Eleanor, I have grown grayer. I am younger than you, you know, but then, what have you to age you? A kind husband, lovely children, while I— I am nothing but a lonely woman. Time goes slowly, slowly for me now.

Why did I never marry? Move that screen a little to one side, please; my eyes can scarcely bear a strong light. Bernard? Oh, that's a long story. I'll tell you if you wish; it might pass an hour.

Do you ever think to go over the old school-days? We thought such foolish things then, didn't we? There wasn't one of us but imagined we would have only to knock ever so faintly on the portals of fame and they would fly wide for our entrance into the magic realms. On Commencement night we whispered merrily among ourselves on the stage to see our favorite planet, Venus, of course, smiling at us through a high, open window, "bidding adieu to her astronomy class," we said.

Then you went away to plunge into the most brilliant whirl of society, and I stayed in the beautiful old city to work.

Bernard was very much *en evidence* those days. He liked you a great deal, because in school-girl parlance you were my "chum." You say,— thanks, no tea, it reminds me that I'm an old maid; you say you know what happiness means — maybe, but I don't think any living soul could experience the joy I felt in those days; it was absolutely painful at times.

Byron and his counterparts are ever dear to the womanly heart, whether young or old. Such a man was he, gloomy, misanthropical, tired of the world, with a few dozen broken love-affairs among his varied experiences. Of course, I worshipped him secretly, what romantic, silly girl of my age, would not, being thrown in such constant contact with him.

One day he folded me tightly in his arms, and said:

"Little girl, I have nothing to give you in exchange for that priceless love of yours but a heart that has already been at another's feet, and a wrecked life, but may I ask for it?"

"It is already yours," I answered. I'll draw the veil over the scene which followed; you know, you've "been there."

Then began some of the happiest hours that ever the jolly old sun beamed upon, or the love-sick moon clothed in her rays of silver. Deceived me? No, no. He admitted that the old love for Blanche was still in his heart, but that he had lost all faith and respect for her, and could nevermore be other than a friend. Well, I was fool enough to be content with such crumbs.

We had five months of happiness. I tamed down beautifully in that time,— even consented to adopt the peerless

Blanche as a model. I gave up all my most ambitious plans and cherished schemes, because he disliked women whose names were constantly in the mouth of the public. In fact, I became quiet, sedate, dignified, renounced too some of my best and dearest friends. I lived, breathed, thought, acted only for him; for me there was but one soul in the universe — Bernard's. Still, for all the suffering I've experienced, I'd be willing to go through it all again just to go over those five months. Every day together, at nights on the lake-shore listening to the soft lap of the waters as the silver sheen of the moon spread over the dainty curled waves; sometimes in a hammock swinging among the trees talking of love and reading poetry. Talk about Heaven! I just think there can't he a better time among the angels.

But there is an end to all things. A violent illness, and his father relenting, sent for the wayward son. I will always believe he loved me, but he was eager to get home to his mother, and anxious to view Blanche in the light of their new relationship. We had a whole series of parting scenes, — tears and vows and kisses exchanged. We clung to each other after the regulation fashion, and swore never to forget, and to write every day. Then there was a final wrench. I went back to my old life— he, away home.

For a while I was content, there were daily letters from him to read ; his constant admonitions to practice ; his many little tokens to adore — until there came a change,— letters less frequent, more mention of Blanche and her love for him, less of his love for me, until the truth was forced upon me. Then I grew cold and proud, and with an iron will crushed and stamped all love for him out of my tortured heart and cried for vengeance.

Yes, quite melo-dramatic, wasn't it? It is a dramatic tale, though.

So I threw off my habits of seclusion and mingled again with men and women, and took up all my long-forgotten plans. It's no use telling you how I succeeded. It was really wonderful, wasn't it? It seems as though that fickle goddess, Fortune, showered every blessing, save one, on my path. Success followed success, triumph succeeded triumph. I was lionized, feted, petted, caressed by the social and literary world. You often used to wonder how I stood it in all those years. God knows; with the heart-sick weariness and the fierce loathing that possessed me, I don't know myself.

But, mind you, Eleanor, I schemed well. I had everything seemingly that humanity craved for, but I suffered, and by all the gods, I swore that he should suffer too. Blanche turned against him and married his brother. An unfortunate chain of circumstances drove him from his father's home branded as a forger. Strange, wasn't it? But money is a strong weapon, and its long arm reaches over leagues and leagues of land and water.

One day he found me in a distant city, and begged for my love again, and for mercy and pity. Blanche was only a mistake, he said, and he loved me alone, and so on. I remembered all his thrilling tones and tender glances, but they might have moved granite now sooner than me. He knelt at my feet and pleaded like a criminal suing for life. I laughed at him and sneered at his misery, and told him what he had done for my happiness, and what I in turn had done for his.

Eleanor, to my dying day, I shall never forget his face as he rose from his knees, and with one awful, indescribable look of hate, anguish and scorn, walked from the room. As he neared the door, all the old love rose in me like a flood, drowning the sorrows of past years, and overwhelming me in a deluge of pity. Strive as I did, I could not repress it; a woman's love is too mighty to be put down with little reasonings. I called to him in terror, "Bernard, Bernard!" He did not turn ; gave no sign of having heard.

"Bernard, come back ; I didn't mean it!"

He passed slowly away with bent head, out of the house and out of my life. I've never seen him since, never heard of him. Somewhere, perhaps on God's earth he wanders outcast, forsaken, loveless. I have my vengeance, but it is like Dead Sea fruit, all bitter ashes to the taste. I am a miserable, heart-weary wreck,— a woman with fame, without love.

"Vengeance is an arrow that often falleth and smiteth the hand of him that sent it."

AT BAY ST. LOUIS.

Soft breezes blow and swiftly show
    Through fragrant orange branches
      parted,
A maiden fair, with sun-flecked hair,
    Caressed by arrows, golden darted.
The vine-clad tree holds forth to me
    A promise sweet of purple blooms,
And chirping bird, scarce seen but
      heard
    Sings dreamily, and sweetly croons
      At Bay St. Louis.

The hammock swinging, idly singing,
    Lissome nut-brown maid
    Swings gaily, freely, to-and-fro ;
The curling, green-white waters casting
      cool, clear shade,
    Rock small, shell boats that go
In circles wide, or tug at anchor's chain,
As though to skim the sea with cargo
      vain,
      At Bay St. Louis.

The maid swings slower, slower to-
and-fro,
And sunbeams kiss gray, dreamy half-
closed eyes;
Fond lover creeping on with foot
steps slow,
Gives gentle kiss, and smiles at sweet
surpise.

* * * * * *

The lengthening shadows tell that eve
is nigh,
And fragrant zephyrs cool and calmer
grow,
Yet still the lover lingers, and scarce
breathed sigh,
Bids the swift hours to pause, nor go,
At Bay St. Louis.

NEW YEAR'S DAY.

———

The poor old year died hard ; for all the
    earth lay cold
    And bare beneath the wintry sky ;
While grey clouds scurried madly to the
    west,
    And hid the chill young moon from
    mortal sight.
Deep, dying groans the aged year
    breathed forth,
    In soughing winds that wailed a re-
    quiem sad
In dull crescendo through the mournful
    air.

———

The new year now is welcomed noisily
    With din and song and shout and
    clanging bell,
And all the glare and blare of fiery fun.
Sing high the welcome to the New Year's
    morn !
    Le roi est mort. Vive, vive le roi !
    cry out,
And hail the new-born king of coming
    days.

———

Alas ! the day is spent and eve draws

nigh;
The king's first subject dies — for
    naught,
And wasted moments by the hundred
    score
Of past years rise like spectres grim
To warn, that these days may not idly
    glide away.
Oh, New Year, youth of promise fair!
    What dost thou hold for me? An
    aching heart?
Or eyes burnt blind by unshed tears?
    Or stabs,
    More keen because unseen?
Nay, nay, dear youth, I've had surfeit
    Of sorrow's feast. The monarch dead
Did rule me with an iron hand. Be
    thou a friend,
    A tender, loving king — and let me
    know
The ripe, full sweetness of a happy year.

THE UNKNOWN LIFE OF JESUS CHRIST.

A new gem has been added to sacred literature, and this is the accidental discovery by Nicolas Notovich of a Buddhist history of a phase of Christ's life left blank in the Scriptures.

Notovich, an adventurer, searching amid the ruins of India, delving deep in all the ancient Buddhistic lore, accidentally stumbles upon the name of Saint Issa, a renowned preacher, ante-dating some 2,000 years. The name becomes a wondrous attraction to Notovich, particularly as he learns through many Buddhist priests, Issa's name in juxtaposition with the Christian faith, and later, has reason to believe that the Jesus Christ of our religion and the Saint Issa of their tradition are identical.

Through a seemingly unfortunate accident, Notovich sustains an injury to his leg, and is cared for most tenderly by the monks of the convent of Himis. Despite his severe agonies, he retains consciousness and curiosity enough to plead for a glimpse of the wonderful documents contained in the archives of the convent, treating of the life of Saint Issa and the genealogy of the House of David. This he has translated and gives to the public.

Just whether to take the history seriously or not is a subject that requires much thought; but whether it be truth or fiction, whether the result of patient investigation and careful study of an interested scholar, or the wild imaginings of a feeble brain, it opens a wild field of speculation to the thoughtful mind.

The first three chapters of this history, contain a brief epitome of the Pentatouch of Moses. Though contrary to the teachings of tradition, Moses is said not to have written these books himself, but that they were transcribed generations after his time. According to this theory, then, the seeming imperfections and inconsistencies and tautological errors of the Old Testament as compared with the brief, clear, concise, logical statement of the Buddhists may readily be explained by the frailty of human memory, and the vividness of Oriental imagination.

Prince Mossa of the Buddhists, otherwise Moses of the Jews, was not, as is popularly supposed, a foundling of the Jews, or a protege of the Egyptian princess, but a full fledged prince, son of Pharoah the mighty. This abrupt overthrow of the tradition of ages is like all disillusions, distasteful, but even the most superficial study of Egyptian customs and laws of that time will serve to impress us with the verity of this opinion. The law of caste was most rigidly and cruelly adhered to, and though all the pleadings and threatenings and weepings of the starry-eyed favorite of the harem may have been brought to bear upon this descendant of Rameses, yet is it probable that a descendant of an outcast race should receive the care and learning and advantages of a legally born prince? Hardly.

The condition of the ancient Israelites in the Christian Scriptures and in the Buddhist parchment are the same, yet there is reason to believe that the former was transcribed many centuries after the hieroglyphics of the latter became faded with age, hence, perhaps, the difference in the parentage of Moses.

"And Mossa was beloved throughout the land of Egypt for the goodness and compassion he displayed for them that suffered, pleaded with his father to soften the lot of these unhappy people, but Pharoah became angry with him, and only imposed more hardships upon his slaves."

At this period in our Scriptures, the Lord communicates with Moses, and inflicts the plagues upon the nation, while in the manuscript of the Himis monks, the annual plague brought on by natural causes falls upon Egypt, and decimates

the community. Here is a strange re-
versal of the order of things. In India,
for ages the home of superstition and
idol worship, that which has always been
regarded by the Christians, the sworn
enemies of the supernatural, as an inexplicable mystery, is accounted for by
perfectly natural causes.

From that time, the fourth chapter of
the chronicle of St. Issa corresponds exactly in its condensed form to the most
prominent chronology of the Old Testament. With the beginning of the next
chapter, the Divine Infant, through
whom the salvation of the world was to
come, appears upon the scene, as the
first born of a poor but highly connected
family, referring, presumably, to the ancestry of Joseph and Mary.

The remarkable wisdom of the child in
earlier years is chronicled in our ancient
parchment with as much care as in the
vellum-bound volume of our church
scriptures. At the age of twelve, the
last glimpse we have of Jesus in the

New Testament, is as a precocious boy, seated in the Temple, expounding the Scriptures to the learned members of the Sanhedrin. After that, we have no further sight of him, until sixteen years later, he re-appears at the marriage in Cana, a grown and serious man, already with well-formulated plans for the furtherance of his father's kingdom. This broad lapse in the Scriptures is filled by one simple sentence in the gospel of St. Luke. "And he was in the desert till the day of his showing into Israel." Where he was, why he had gone, and what he was doing are left to the imagination of the scholar and commentator.

Many theories have been advanced, and the one most accepted, was that he had followed the trade of his terrestrial father, Joseph, and was near Jerusalem among the tools of carpentry, helping his parents to feed the hungry mouths of his brothers and sisters.

But there appears another plausible theory advanced by the Buddhist histo-

rians, and sustained by the Buddhist
traditions, that as Moses had fled into
the wilderness to spend forty years in
fasting and preparation for his life work,
so Jesus had fled, not to the wilderness,
but to the ancient culture and learning
and the wisdom of centuries to prepare
himself, by a knowledge of all religions
for the day of the redemption.

Among the Jews of that day, and even
among the more conservative descend-
ants of Abraham yet, there existed, and
exists a law which accustoms the marrying of the sons, especially the oldest son,
at the age of thirteen. It is supposed
that Issa, resisting the thraldom and carnal temptation of the marital state, fled
from the importunities of the wise men,
who would fain unite their offspring with
such a wise and serious youth.

" It was then that Issa clandestinely
left his father's house, went out of Jerusalem, and in company with some mer-
chants, travelled toward Sinai."

" That he might perfect himself in the

divine word and study the laws of the Great Buddha."

For six years he kept all India stirred to its utmost depths as he afterward kept all Palestine stirred by the purity of his doctrines, and the direct simplicity of his teachings. The white priests of Bramah gave him all their law, teaching him the language and religion of the dwellers of the five rivers. In Juggernaut, Rajegrilia, Benares, and other holy cities he was beloved by all. For true, here, as elsewhere, to his theory of the universal brotherhood of man, not only did he move among the upper classes, but also with the wretched Vaisyas and Soudras, the lowest of low castes who even were forbidden to hear the Vedas read, save only on feast days. Just as among the Jews, he was tolerant, merciful and kindly disposed towards the Samaritans, the Magdalens, the Lazaruses as to the haughty rabbis.

His impress upon the home of Buddha and Brahma was manifested by the hitherto unknown theory of monontheism, established by him, but gradually permitted to fall into desuetude, and become confounded with the polytheistic hierarchy of the confusing religion. Just as the grand oneness and simplicity of the Christian religion has been permitted to deterioate into many petty sects, each with its absurd limitations, and its particular little method of worshipping the Great Father.

The teachings of Issa in India bear close relation in the general trend of thought to the teachings of Jesus among the multitudes about Jerusalem. There is the same universal simplicity of man's brotherhood ; the complete self-abnegation of the flesh to the mind; the charitable impulses of a kind heart, and the utter disregard of caste, whether of birth, or breeding, or riches.

Of miracles in India, Issa says, " The miracles of our God began when the universe was created, they occur each day, each instant ; whosoever does not see them, is deprived of one of the most beautiful gifts of life."

At last, according to the chronicles of the Buddhists, Issa was recalled from his labors in India to the land of Israel, where the people oppressed as of old by the Pharoahs, and now by the mighty men from the country of the Ramones, otherwise the Romans.

Here Pilate appears in a new light. Heretofore he has always been a passive figure in the story of the crucifixion. Indeed he is enrirely exonerated from all blame by some of our religious bibliographers and made to appear in a philanthrophic light, but the priests of Egypt, undeceived by the treacherous memories and careless chronicling on the disciples of old, place Pilate before us as a thorough Roman, greedy, crafty, cruel, unscrupulous. According to them he places, a spy upon the actions of Jesus in the beginning of his three years teachings, who follows him in all his journeys, and in the end betrays him to the Romans. This person can be no other than Judas, the betrayer. And here we are permitted to view his seemingly inexplicable actions in a new light, and from being Judas, a sorrowing misanthrope, the erst-while friend of Christ, he becomes merely a common enemy, the tool of the Romans.

Then we have the trial and death of Issa, strongly similar to our accepted version, and the chronicle briefly ends with the statement of the subsequent work of the desciples. The story of the Buddist was written very shortly after the Passion of the Cross; the New Testament was transcribed years after the chief actors were dust.

We are so steeped in tradition, and so conservative on any subject that touches our religious beliefs that it is somewhat difficult to reconcile ourselves to another addition to our Scriptures. But if we should look at the matter earnestly, and give deep thought to the relative positions, lives, and endings of these two noble men, Issa and Christ, we could scarcely doubt that they are one. Without trying, as does the author, to break down with one fell swoop, the entire structure of the Bible, we cannot but admit the probality of the new theory.

It may be claimed that the remarkable personality of Christ would have left more of an impress upon India than it did, and that Christianity there and in India would have been synchronous, but we must remember, that there among the idols of Bramah and Vishnu, the way was not prepared, the people unexpectant of a new prophet, unwarned of him and unheeded. There he seems to have had no close personal followers to take up the work just where he left it, and continue. The dwellers of India were more happy in their entirety and more comfortable than the Jews, hence there was no Deliverer to impress them forever with the gigantic sacrifice of human frame and Divine soul.

St. Issa, one of the most revered prophets of the Buddists, Jesus Christ,

the Man and God of all other men, the
divine incarnation of the ideal, are they
the same? Why not?

IN OUR NEIGHBORHOOD.

The Harts were going to give a party.
Neither Mrs. Hart, nor the Misses Hart,
nor the small and busy Harts who
amused themselves and the neighborhood
by continually falling in the gutter on
special occasions, had mentioned this fact
to anyone, but all the interested denizens
of that particlar square could tell by the
unusual air of bustle and activity which
pervaded the Hart domicile. Lillian,
the æsthetic, who furnished theme for
many spirited discussions, leaned airily
out of the window; her auburn (red)

tresses carefully done in curl papers. Martha, the practical, flourished the broom and duster with unwonted activity, which the small boys of the neighborhood, peering through the green shutters of the front door, duly reported to their mammas, busily engaged in holding down their respective door-steps by patiently sitting thereon.

Pretty soon, the junior Harts,— two in number — began to travel to and fro, soliciting the loan of a " few chairs," " some nice dishes," and such like things, indispensable to every decent, self-respecting party. But to all inquiries as to the use to which these articles were to be put, they only vouchsafed one reply, " Ma told us as we wasn't to tell, just ask for the things, that's all."

Mrs. Tuckley the dress-maker, brought her sewing out on the front-steps, and entered a vigorous protest to her next-door neighbor.

" Humph," she sniffed, " mighty funny they can't say what's up. Must be something in it. Couldn't get none o' *my* things, and not invite *me*!"

"Did she ask you for any?" absent-mindedly inquired Mrs. Luke, shielding her eyes from the sun.

"No-o—, but she'd better sense, she knows *me*—she ain't—mercy me, Stella! Just look at that child tumbling in the mud! You, Stella, come here, I say! Look at you now, there—and there—and there?"

The luckless Stella having been soundly cuffed, and sent whimpering in the back-yard, Mrs. Tuckley continued,

"Yes as I was saying, 'course, taint none o' my business, but I always did wonder how them Harts do keep up. Why, them girls dress just as fine as any lady on the Avenue and that there Lillian wears real diamond ear-rings. 'Pears mighty, mighty funny to me, and Lord the airs they do put on! Holdin' up their heads like nobody's good enough to speak to. I don't like to talk about people, you know, yourself, Mrs. Luke I never speak about anybody, but mark my word, girls that cut up capers like them Hartses' girls never come to any good."

Mrs. Luke heaved a deep sigh of appreciation at the wisdom of her neighbor, but before she could reply a re-inforcement in the person of little Mrs. Peters, apron over her head, hands shrivelled and soap-sudsy from washing, appeared.

"Did you ever see the like?" she asked in her usual, rapid breathless way. "Why, my Louis says they're putting canvass cloths on the floor, and taking down the bed in the back-room; and putting greenery and such like trash about. Some style about them, eh?"

Mrs. Tuckley tossed her head and sniffed contemptously, Mrs. Luke began to rehearse a time worn tale, how once a carriage had driven up to the Hart house at nine o'clock at night, and a distinguished looking man alighted, went in, stayed about ten minutes and finally drove off with a great clatter. Heads that had shaken ominously over this story before began to shake again, and tongues that had wagged themselves tired with conjectures started now with some brand new ideas and theories. The children of the square, tired of fishing for minnows in the ditches, and making mudpies in the street, clustered about their mother's skirts receiving occasional slaps, when their attempts at taking part in the conversation became too pronounced.

Meanwhile, in the Hart household, all was bustle and preparation. To and fro the members of the house flitted, arranging chairs, putting little touches here and there, washing saucers and glasses, chasing the Hart Juniors about, loosing things and calling frantically for each other's assistance to find them. Mama Hart, big, plump and perspiring, puffed here and there like a large, rosy engine, giving impossible orders, and receiving sharp answers to foolish questions. Lillian, the æsthetic, practiced her most graceful poses before the large mirror in the parlor ; Martha rushed about, changing the order of the furniture, and Papa Hart, just come in from work, paced the rooms disconsolately, asking for dinner.

"Dinner!" screamed Mama Hart, "Dinner, who's got time to fool with dinner this evening ? Look in the sideboard and you'll see some bread and ham; eat that and shut up."

Eight o'clock finally arrived, and with it, the music and some straggling guests. When the first faint chee-chee of the violin floated out into the murky atmosphere, the smaller portion of the neighborhood went straightway into ectasies. Boys and girls in all stages of deshabille clustered about the door-steps and gave vent to audible exclamations of approval or disapprobation concerning the state of affairs behind the green shutters. It was a warm night and the big round moon sailed serenely in a cloudless, blue sky. Mrs. Tuckley had put on a clean calico wrapper, and planted herself with the indomitable Stella on her steps, "to watch the purceedings."

The party was a grand success. Even the intensely critical small fry dancing on the pavement without to the scraping and fiddling of the string band, had to admit that. So far as they were concenred it was all right, but what shall we say of the guests within? They who glided easily over the canvassed floors, bowed, and scraped and simpered, "just like the big folks on the Avenue," who ate the ice-cream and cake, and drank the sweet, weak Catawba wine amid boisterous healths to Mr. and Mrs. Hart and the Misses Hart; who smirked and perspired and cracked ancient jokes and heart-rending puns during the intervals of the dances, who shall say that they did not enjoy themselves as thoroughly and as fully as those who frequented the wealth-ier entertainments up-town.

Lillian and Martha in gossamer gowns of pink and blue flitted to and fro attend-ing to the wants of their guests. Mrs.

Hart, gorgeous in a black satin affair, all folds and lace and drapery, made desperate efforts to appear cool and collected — and failed miserably. Papa Hart spent one half his time standing in front of the mantle, spreading out his coat-tails, and benignly smiling upon the young people, while the other half was devoted to initiating the male portion of the guests into the mysteries of "snake killing."

Everybody had said that he or she had had a splendid time, and finally, when the last kisses had been kissed, the last good-byes been said, the whole Hart family sat down in the now deserted and disordered rooms, and sighed with relief that the great event was over at last.

"Nice crowd, eh?" remarked Papa Hart. He was brimful of joy and second-class whiskey, so no one paid any attention to him.

"But did you see how shamefully Maude flirted with Willie Howard? said Lillian. Martha tossed her head in disdain ; Mr. Howard she had always considered her especial property, so Lillian's observation had a rather disturbing effect.

." I'm so warm and tired," cried Mama Hart, plaintively, " children how are we going to sleep to-night?"

Thereupon the whole family arose to devise ways and means for wooing the drowsy god. As for the Hart Juniors they had long since solved the problem by falling asleep with sticky hands and faces upon a pile of bed-clothing behind the kitchen door.

———

It was late in the next day before the house had begun to resume anything like its former appearance. The little Harts were kept busy all morning returning chairs and dishes, and distributing the remnants of the feast to the vicinity. The ice-cream had melted into a warm custard, and the cakes had a rather worse for wear appearance, but they were appreciated as much as though just from the confectioner. No one was forgotten, even Mrs. Tuckley, busily stitching on a muslin garment on the steps, and unctuously rolling the latest morsel of scandal under her tongue, was obliged to confess that "them Hartses wasn't such bad people after all, just a bit queer at times."

About two o'clock, just as Lillian was re-draping the tidies on the stiff, common plush chairs in the parlor, some one pulled the bell violently. The visitor, a rather good-looking young fellow, with a worried expression smiled somewhat sarcastically as he heard a sound of scuffling and running within the house.

———

Presently Mrs. Hart opened the door wiping her hand, red and smoking with dish-water, upon her apron. The worried expression deepended on the visitor's face as he addressed the woman with visible embarrasment.

"Er- I - I - suppose you are Mrs. Hart?"

he inquired awkwardly.

" That's my name, sir," replied she with pretentous dignity.

"Er - your-er - may I come in madam ?"

" Certainly," and she opened the door to admit him, and offered a chair.

" Your husband is an employee in the Fisher Oil Mills, is he not ? "

Mrs. Hart straightened herself with pride as she replied in the affirmative. She had always been proud of Mr. Hart's position as foreman of the big oil mills, and was never so happy as when he was expounding to some one in her presence, the difficulties and intricacies of machine-work.

" Well you see my dear Mrs. Hart," continued the visitor. " Now pray don't get excited— there has been an accident, and you're husband— has-er - been hurt, you know."

But for a painful whitening in her usu-ally rosy face, and a quick compression of her lips, the wife made no sign.

" What was the accident?" she queried,

leaning her elbows on her knees.

"Well, you see, I don't understand machinery and the like, but there was something about a wheel out of gear, and a band bursted, or something, anyhow a big wheel flew to pieces, and as he was standing near, he was hit."

"Where?"

"Well — well, I may as well tell you the truth, madam ; a large piece of the wheel struck him on the head— and — he was killed instantly."

She did not faint, nor make any outcry, nor tear her hair as he had partly expected, but sat still staring at him, with a sort a helpless, dumb horror shining out her eyes, then with a low moan, bowed her head on her knees and shuddered, just as Lillian came in, curious to know what the handsome stranger had to say to her mother.

———

The poor mutilated body came home at last, and was laid in a stiff, silver-decorated, black coffin in the middle of the sitting-room, which had been made to look as uncomfortable and unnatural as mirrors and furniture shrouded in sheets and mantel and tables divested of ornaments would permit.

There was a wake that night to the unconfined joy of the neighbors, who would rather a burial than a wedding. The friends of the family sat about the coffin, and through the house with long pulled faces. Mrs. Tuckley officiated in the kitchen, making coffee and dispensing cheese and crackers to those who were hungry. As the night wore on, and the first restraint disappeared, jokes were cracked, and quiet laughter indulged in, while the young folks congregated in the kitchen, were hilariously happy, until some member of the family would appear, when every face would sober down.

The older persons contented themselves with recounting the virtues of the deceased, and telling anecdotes wherein he figured largely. It was astonishing how many intimate friends of his had suddenly come to light. Every other man present had either attended school with him, or was a close companion until he died. Proverbs and tales and witty sayings were palmed off as having emanated from his lips. In fact, the dead man would have been surprised himself, had he suddenly come to life and discovered what an important, what a modern solomon he had become.

The long night dragged on, and the people departed in groups of twos and threes, until when the gray dawn crept slowly over the blackness of night shrouding the electric lights in mists of cloudy blue, and sending cold chills of dampness through the house, but a few of the great crowd remained.

The day seemed so gray in contrast to the softening influence of the nigh, the grief which could be hidden then, must now come forth and parade itself before all eyes. There was the funeral to prepare for ; the dismal black dresses

and bonnets with their long crape veils
to don; there were the condolences of
sorrowing friends to receive; the floral
offerings to be looked at. The little
Harts strutted about resplendent in stiff
black cravats, and high crape bands
about their hats. They were divided
between two conflicting emotions—joy
at belonging to a family so noteworthy
and important, and sorrow at the death.
As the time for the funeral approached,
and Lillian began to indulge in a series
of fainting fits, the latter feeling predom-
inated.

———-

"Well it was all over at last, the
family had returned, and as on two nights
previous, sat once more in the deserted
and dismantled parlor. Mrs. Tuckley
and Mrs. Luke, having rendered all assistance possible, had repaired to their
respective front steps to keep count of
the number of visitors who returned to
condole with the family.

"A real nice funeral," remarked the

dress-maker at last, " a nice funeral.
Everybody took it so hard, and Lillian
fainted real beautiful. She's a good girl
that Lillian. Poor things, I wonder what
they'll do now."

Stella, the irrepressible, was busily engaged balancing herself on one toe, *a la*
ballet.

" Mebbe she's goin' to get married,"
she volunteered eagerly, " 'cos I saw that
yeller-haired young man what comes
there all the time, wif his arms around
her waist, and a tellin' her not to grieve
as he'd take care of her. I was a peepin'
in the dinin'-room."

" How dare you peep at other folks,
and pry into people's affairs? I can't im-
agine where you get your meddlesome
ways from. There aint none in *my
family.* Next time I catch you at it,
I'll spank you good." Then, after a
pause, "Well what else did he say?"

FAREWELL.

Farewell, sweetheart, and again farewell;
To day we part, and who can tell
  If we shall e'er again
Meet, and with clasped hands
Renew our vows of love, and forget
  The sad, dull pain.

Dear heart, 'tis bitter thus to lose thee
And think mayhap, you will forget me ;
  And yet, I thrill
As I remember long and happy days
Fraught with sweet love and pleasant
    memories
  That linger still

You go to loved ones who will smile
And clasp you in their arms, and all the
    while
  I stay and moan
For you, my love, my heart and strive
To gather up life's dull, gray thread
  And walk alone.

Aye, with you love the red and gold

Goes from my life, and leaves it cold
 And dull and bare,
Why should I strive to live and learn
And smile and jest, and daily try
 You from my heart to tare?

Nay, sweetheart, rather would I lie
Me down, and sleep for aye; or fly
 To regions far
Where cruel Fate is not and lovers live
Nor feel the grim, cold hand of Destiny
 Their way to bar.

I murmur not, dear love, I only say
Again farewell. God bless the day
 On which we met,
And bless you too, my love, and be with
 you
In sorrow or in happiness, nor let you
 E'er me forget.

LITTLE MISS SOPHIE.

When Miss Sophie knew consciousness again, the long, faint, swelling notes
of the organ were dying away in distant
echoes through the great arches of the
silent church, and she was alone, crouching in a little, forsaken, black heap at the
altar of the Virgin.   The twinkling tapers
seemed to smile pityingly upon her, the
beneficent   smile   of   the   white-robed
Madonna seemed to whisper comfort.
A long gust of chill air swept up the
aisles, and Miss Sophie shivered, not
from cold, but from nervousness.

But darkness was failing, and soon
the lights would be lowered, and the
great, massive doors would be closed,
so gathering her thin little cape about
her frail shoulders, Miss Sophie hurried
out, and along the brilliant noisy streets
home.

It was a wretched, lonely little room,
where the cracks let the boisterous wind

whistle through, and the smoky, grimy walls looked cheerless and unhomelike. A miserable little room in a miserable little cottage in one of the squalid streets of the Third District that nature and the city fathers seemed to have forgotten.

As bare and comfortless the room, so was Miss Sophie's lonely life. She rented these four walls from an unkempt little Creole woman, whose progeny seemed like the promised offspring of Abraham, — multitudinous, The flickering life in the pale little body she scarcely kept there by the unceasing toil of a pair of bony hands, stitching, stitching, ceaselessly, wearingly on the bands and pockets of pants. It was her bread, this monotonous, unending work, and though while days and nights constant labor brought but the most meagre recompense, it was her only hope of life.

She sat before the little charcoal brazier and warmed her transparent, needle-pricked fingers, thinking meanwhile of the strange events of the day. She had been up town to carry the great, black bundle of pants and vests to the factory and receive her small pittance, and on the way home stopped in at the Jesuit Church to say her little prayer at the altar of the calm, white Virgin. There had been a wondrous burst of music from the great organ as she knelt there, an overpowering perfume of many flowers, the glittering dazzle of many lights, and the dainty frou-frou of silken skirts of wedding guests filing and tripping. So Miss Sophie stayed to the wedding, for what feminine heart, be it ever so old and seared, does not delight in one? And why should'nt a poor little Creole old maid be interested too?

When the wedding party had filed in solemnly, to the rolling, swelling, pealing tones of the organ. Important-looking groomsmen, dainty, fluffy, white-robed maids, stately, satin-robed, illusion-veiled bride, and happy groom. She leaned forward to catch a better glimpse of their faces.   Ah!—

Those near the Virgin's altar who heard a faint sigh and rustle on the steps glanced curiously as they saw a slight, black-robed figure clutch the railing and lean her head against it.   Miss Sophie had fainted.

"I must have been hungry," she mused over the charcoal fire in her little room, "I must have been hungry," and she smiled a wan smile, and busied herself getting her evening meal of coffee and bread and ham.

If one were given to pity, the first thought that would rush to one's lips at sight of Miss Sophie would have been : Poor little Miss Sophie!   She had come among the bareness and sordidness of this neighborhood five years ago, robed in crepe, and crying with great sobs that seemed to fairly shake the vitality out of her.   Perfectly silent, too, about her former life, but for all that, Michel, the quarter grocer at the corner, and Mme. Laurent, who kept the rabbe shop oppo-

site, had fixed it all up between them, of
her sad history and past glories. Not
that they knew, but then Michel must
invent something when the neighbors
came to him, their fountain head of
wisdom.

One morning little Miss Sophie
opened wide her dingy windows to
catch the early freshness of the autumn
wind as it whistled through the yellow-
leafed trees. It was one of those, calm,
blue-misted, balmy, November days that
New Orleans can have when all the rest
of the country is fur-wrapped. Miss
Sophie pulled her machine to the window, where the sweet, damp wind ·could
whisk among her black locks.

Whirr, whirr, went the machine, tick-
ing fast and lightly over the belts of the
rough jean pants. Whirr, whirr, yes,
and Miss Sophie was actually humming
a tune! She felt strangely light to-day.

" *Ma foi*," muttered Michel, strolling
across the street to where Mme. Laurent
sat sewing behind the counter on blue

and brown-checked aprons, " but the little ma'amselle sings. Perhaps she recollects."

" Perhaps," muttered the rabbe woman.

But little Miss Sophie felt restless. A strange impulse seemed drawing her up town, and the machine seemed to run slow, slow, before it would stitch the endless number of jean belts. Her fingers trembled with nervous haste as she pinned up the unwieldy black bundle of the finished work, and her feet fairly tripped over each other in their eagerness to get to Claiborne Street, where she could board the up-town car. There was a feverish desire to go somewhere, a sense of elation,— foolish happiness that brought a faint echo of color into her pinched cheeks. She wondered why.

No one noticed her in the car. Passengers on the Claiborne line are too much accustomed to frail, little black-robed women with big, black bundles; it is one of the city's most pitiful sights.

She leaned her head out of the window to catch a glimpse of the oleanders on Bayou Road, when her attention was caught by a conversation in the car.

"Yes; it's too bad for Neale, and lately married too," said the elder man, "I can't see what he is to do."

Neale! she pricked up her ears. That was the name of the groom in the Jesuit church.

"How did it happen?" languidly inquired the younger. He was a stranger, evidently; a stranger with a high regard for the faultlessness of male attire, too.

"Well, the firm failed first; he didn't mind that much, he was so sure of his uncle's inheritance repairing his lost fortunes, but suddenly this difficulty of identification springs up, and he is literally on the verge of ruin."

"Won't some of you fellows who've known him all your lives do to identify him?"

"Gracious man, we've tried, but the absurd old will expressly stipulates that he shall be known only by a certain quaint Roman ring, and unless he has it — no identification, no fortune. He has given the ring away and that settles it."

"Well, you're all chumps. Why doesn't he get the ring from the owner?"

"Easily said — but — It seems that Neale had some little Creole love-affair some years ago and gave this ring to his dusky-eyed fiancee. But you how Neale is with his love-affairs, went off and forgot the girl in a month. It seems, however, she took it to heart,— so much so until he's ashamed to try to find her or the ring."

Miss Sophie heard no more as she gazed out into the dusty grass. There were tears in her eyes, hot blinding ones that wouldn't drop for pride, but stayed and scalded. She knew the story with all its embellishments of heartaches. The ring, too ; she remembered the day she had kissed and wept and fondled it, until it seemed her heart must burst under its load of grief before she took it to the pawn broker's that another might be eased before the end came,— that other, her father. The "little Creole love affair" of Neale's had not always been poor and old and jaded-looking; but reverses must come, even Neale knew that. — so the ring was at the *Mont de Piete.*

Still he must have it, it was his; it would save him from disgrace and suffering, and from trailing the proud head of the white-gowned bride into sorrow. He must have it,— but how?

There it was still at the pawn-broker's, no one would have such a jewel, and the ticket was home in the bureau drawer. Well, he must have it; she might starve in the attempt. Such a thing as going to him and telling him that he might redeem it was an impossibility. That good, straight-backed, stiff-necked Creole blood would have risen in all its strength and choked her. No; as a present had the quaint Roman circlet been placed upon her finger,— as a present should it be returned.

The bumping car rode heavily, and
the hot thoughts beat heavily in her poor
little head. He must have the ring —
but how — the ring — the Roman ring
— the white-robed bride starving — she
was going mad — ah yes, — the church.

Right in the busiest, most bustling
part of the town, its fresco and bronze
and iron quaintly suggestive of mediæval times. Within, all cool and dim and
restful, with the faintest whiff of lingering incense rising and pervading the
gray arches. Yes, the Virgin would
know and have pity; the sweet, white-
robed Virgin at the pretty flower-decked
altar, or the one away up in the niche,
far above the golden dome where the
Host was. Holy Mary, Mother of God.
Poor little Miss Sophie.

Titiche, the busy-body of the house,
noticed that Miss Sophie's bundle was
larger than usual that afternoon. " Ah,
poor woman ! " sighed Titiche's mother,
" she would be rich for Christmas."

The bundle grew larger each day, and

Miss Sophie grew smaller. The damp, cold rain and mist closed the white-curtained window, but always there behind the sewing machine drooped and bobbed the little black-robed figure. Whirr, whirr went the wheels, and the coarse jean pants piled in great heaps at her side. The Claiborne street car saw her oftener than before, and the sweet, white Virgin in the flowered niche above the gold-domed altar smiled at the little penitent almost every day.

" *Ma foi*," said the slatternly land lady to Madame Laurent and Michel one day, "I no see how she live! Eat? Nothing, nothing, almost, and las' night when it was so cold and foggy, eh? I hav' to mek him build fire She mos' freeze."

Whereupon the rumor spread that Miss Sophie was starving herself to death to get some luckless relative out of jail for Christmas, — a rumor which enveloped her scraggy little figure with a kind of halo to the neighbors when she appeared on the streets.

November had verged into December
and the little pile of coins were yet far
from the sum needed. Dear God! how
the money did have to go. The rent,
and the groceries and the coal,— though,
to be sure, she used a precious bit of
that. All the work and saving and
skimping,— maybe, yes, maybe by Christmas. What a gift!

Christmas Eve night on Royal Street
is ro place for a weakling, for the shouts
and carousals of the roisterers will strike
fear into the brave. Yet amid the cries
and yells, the deafening blow of horns
and tin whistles and the really dangerous
fusilade of fireworks, the little figure
hurried along, one hand cluthching tight
the battered hat that the rude merry-
makers would have torn off, the other
grasping under the thin, black cape a
worn little pocketbook.

Into the *Mont de Piete*, breathless,
eager. The ticket? Here, worn, crumpled. The ring? It was not gone?
No, thank Heaven! It was really a joy

well worth her toil, she thought, to have it again.

Had Titiche not been shooting crackers on the banquette instead of peering into the crack, as was his wont, his big, round, black eyes would have grown saucer-wide to see little Miss Sophie kiss and fondle a ring, an ugly clumsy band of gold.

"Ah, dear ring," she murmured, once you were his, and you shall be his again. You shall be on his finger, and perhaps touch his heart. Dear ring, *ma chere petite, de ma coeur, cheri, de ma coeur. Je t'aime, je t'aime, oui, oui.* You are his, youwere mine once too. To-night, just one night, I'll keep you — then — to-morrow, where you can save him.

Ah, thé Virgin — she smiles at me because I did right, did I not sweet mother? She smiles — and — I grow — faint — "

The loud whistles and horns of the little ones rose on the balmy air next morning. No one would doubt it was Christmas Day, even if doors and windows are open wide to let in cool air.

Why, there was Christmas even in the very look of the mules on the poky cars ; there was Christmas noise in the streets, and Christmas toys and Christmas odors, savory ones that made the nose wrinkle approvingly, issuing from the kitchen. Michel and Mme. Laurent smiled greetings across the street at each other, and the salutation from a passer-by recalled the many progenied landlady to herself.

" Miss Sophie, well, poor soul, not very much Christmas for her. *Mais*, I'll just call her in to spend the day with me.   It'll cheer her a bit."

So clean and orderly within the poor little room   Not a speck of dust or a litter of any kind on the quaint little old-time high bureau, unless you might except a sheet of paper lying loose with something written on it.   Titiche had evidently inherited his prying propensities for the landlady turned it over and read :

" Louis.   Here is the ring.   I return

it to you.   I heard you needed it, I hope
it comes not too late.   Sophie."

"The ring, where?" muttered the
landlady.   There it was, clasped between
her fingers on her bosom.   A bosom,
white and cold, under a cold, happy face.
Christmas had indeed dawned for Miss
Sophie—the eternal Christmas.

IF I HAD KNOWN.

If I had known
Two years ago how drear this life should
     be,
And crowd upon itself allstrangely sad,
Mayhap another song would burst from
     out my lips,
Overflowing with the happiness of future
     hopes;
Mayhap another throb than that of joy,
Have stirred my soul into its inmost
     depths,
               If I had known.

If I had known,
Two years ago the impotence of love,
The vainness of a kiss, how barren a
    caress,
Mayhap my soul to higher things have
    soarn,
Nor clung to earthly loves and tender
    dreams,
But ever up aloft into the blue empyrean,
And there to master all the world of
    mind,
                If I had known.

CHALMETLE.

Wreaths of lilies and immortelles,
Scattered upon each silent mound,
Voices in loving remembrance swell,
Chanting to heaven the solemn sound.
Glad skies above, and glad earth beneath;
And grateful hearts who silently
Gather earth's flowers, and tenderly
    wreath

Woman's sweet token of fragility.

Ah, the noble forms who fought so well
Lie, some unnamed, 'neath the grassy
    mound;
Heroes, brave heroes, the stories tell,
Silently too, the unmarked mounds,
Tenderly wreath them about with flowers,
Joyously pour out your praises loud ;
For every joy beat in these hearts of
    ours
Is only a drawing us nearer to God.

Little enough is the song we sing,
Little enough is the tale we tell,
When we think of the voices who erst
    did ring
Ere their owners in smoke of battle fell.
Little enough are the flowers we cull
To scatter afar on the grass-grown
    graves,
When we think of bright eyes, now
    d mmed and dull
For the cause they loyally strove to save.

And they fought right well, did these
    brave men,

For their banner still floats unto the
    breeze,
And the pæans of ages forever shall tell
Their glorious tale beyond the seas.
Ring out your voices in praises loud,
Sing sweet your notes of music gay,
Tell me in all you loyal crowd
Throbs there a heart unmoved to-day ?

Meeting together again this year,
As met we in fealty and love before ;
Men, maids, and matrons to reverent'y
    hear
Praises of brave men who fought of yore.
Tell to the little ones with wondering
    eyes,
The tale of the flag that floats so free ;
Till their tiny voices shall merrily rise
In hymns of rejoicing and praises to Thee.

Many a pure and noble heart
Lies under the sod, all covered with
    green ;
Many a soul that had felt the smart
Of life's sad torture, or mayhap had
    seen

The faint hope of love pass afar from
    the sight,
    Like swift flight of bird to a rarer clime
Many a youth whose death caused the
    blight
Of tender hearts in that long, sad time.

Nay, but this is no hour for sorrow ;
They died at their duty, shall we repine ?
Let us gaze hopefully on to the morrow
Praying that our lives thus shall shine.
Ring out your bugles, sound out your
    cheers !
Man has been God-like so may we be.
Give cheering thanks, there dry up those
    tears,
Widowed and orphaned, the country is
    free !

Wreathes of lillies and immortelles,
Scattered upon each silent mound,
Voices in loving remembrance swell,
Chanting to heaven the solemn sound,
Glad skies above, and glad earth beneath,
And grateful hearts who silently
Gather earth's flowers, and tenderly
    wreath
Woman's sweet token of fragility.

AT EVENTIDE.

——

All day had she watched and waited for his coming, and still her strained ears caught no sounds of the footsteps she loved and longed to hear. All day while the great sun panted on his way around the brazen skies; all day while the busy world throbbed its mighty engines of labor, nor witted of the breaking hearts in its midst. And now when the eve had come, and the sun sank slowly to rest, casting his red rays over the earth he loved, and bidding tired nature a gentle radiant good-night, she still watched and waited. Waited while the young moon shone silvery in the crimson flush of the eastern sky, while the one bright star trembled as he strove to near his love; waited while the hum of soul-wearing traffic died in the distant streets, and the merry voices of happy children floated to her ears.

And still he came not. What kept him from her side? Had he learned the cold lesson of self-control, or found one other thing more potent than love? Had some cruel chain of circumstances forced him to disobey her bidding — or — did he love another? But no, she smiles triumphantly, he could not having known and loved her.

Sitting in the deep imbrasure of the window through which the distant wave sounds of city life floated to her, the pages of her life seemed to turn back, and she read the almost forgotten tale of long ago, the story of their love. In those days his wish had been her law; his smile her sun ; his frown her wretchedness. Within his arms, earth seemed a far-away dream of empty nothingness, and when his lips touched and clung to hers, sweet with the perfume of the South they floated away into a Paradise of enfolding space, where Time and Death and the woes of this great earth are naught, only these two — and love, the almighty.

And so their happiness drifted slowly across the sea of Time until it struck a cruel rock, whose sharp teeth showed not above the dimpled waves; and where once had been a craft of strength and beauty, now was only a hideous wreck. For the Tempter had come into this Eden, and soon his foul whisper found place in her heart.

And the Tempter's name was Ambition.

Often had the praises and plaudits of men rang in her ears when her sweet voice sang to her chosen friends, often had the tears evoked by her songs of love and hope and trust, thrilled her breast faintly, as the young bird stirs in its nest under the loving mother's wing, but he had clasped his arms around her, and that was enough. But one day the Tempter whispered, "Why waste such talent; bring that beauty of voice before the world and see men bow in homage, and women envy and praise. Come forth and follow me."

But she put him fiercely aside, and cried, " I want no homage but his, I want no envy from any one."

Still the whisper stayed in her heart, nor would the honeyed words of praise be gone, even when he kissed her, and thanked the gods for this pearl of great price.

Then as time fled on, the tiny whisper grew into a great roar, and all the praise of men, and the sweet words of women, filled her brain, and what had once been her aversion became a great desire, and caused her brow to grow thoughtful, and her eyes moody.

But when she spoke to him of this new love, he smiled and said, "My wife must be mine, and mine alone. I want not a woman whom the world claims, and shouts her name abroad. My wife and my home must by inviolate." And again as of yore, his wish controlled her — but only for a while.

Then the tiny whisper grown into the

great roar urging her on, became a mighty wind which drove her before it, nor could she turn aside from the path of ambition, but swept on, and conquered.

Ah, sweet, sweet the exultation of the victor! Dear the plaudits of the admiring world; wild the joy, when queen of song, admired of men, she stood upon the pinacle of fame! And he? True to his old convictions, turned sadly from the woman who placed the admiration of the world before his love and the happiness of his home — and went out from her life broken-hearted, disappointed, miserable.

All these things, and more, she thought upon in the first flush of eventide, as the bold, young star climbed toward his lady-love, the moon, all these things, and what had come to pass after the victory.

For there came a day when the world wearied of its toy, and turned with shouts of joy, and wreaths of fresh laurels for the new star. Then came disappointments and miseries crowding fast upon her; the sorrows which a loving heart knows when its finds its idols faithless. Then the love for him which she had once repressed arose in all its strength which had gained during the long struggle with the world, arose and overwhelmed her with its might, and filled her soul with an unutterable longing for peace and rest and him.

She wrote to him and told him all her heart, and begged of him to come back to her, for Fame was but an empty bubble while love was supreme and the only happiness, after all. And now she waited while the crimson and gold of the west grew dark, and gray and lowering.

Hark! She hears his loved step. He comes, ah, joy of heaven he comes! Soon will he clasp her in his arms, and there on his bosom shall she know peace and rest and love.

As he enters the door she hastens to meet him, the love-light shining in her tired eyes, her soft rounded arms outstretched to meet him. But he folds her not in his embrace, nor yet does he look with love into her upturned eyes; the voice she loves, ah so well, breaks upon the dusky silence, pitiless, stern.

"Most faithless of faithless women, think you that like the toy of a fickle child I can be thrown aside, then picked up again? Think you that I can take a soiled lily to my bosom? Think you that I can cherish the gaudy sun-flower that ever turns to the broad, brazen glare of the uncaring sun, rather than the modest shrinking, violet? Nay, be not deceived, I loved you once, but that love you killed in its youth and beauty leaving me to stand and weep alone over its grave. I came to-night, not to kiss you, and to forgive you as you entreat, but to tell that you I have wed another."

The pitiless voice ceased, and she was alone in the dusky silence; alone in all the shame and agony and grief of unrequited love and worthless fame. Alone to writhe and groan in despair while the roseate flush of eventide passed into the coldness of midnight.

Oh faithless woman, oh, faithless man! How frail the memory of thy binding vows, thy blissful hours of love! Are they forgotten? Only the record of broken hearts and loveless lives will show.

———-

THE IDLER.

———

An idle lingerer on the wayside's road,
He gathers up his work and yawns away;
A little longer, ere the tiresome load
Shall be reduced to ashes or to clay.

No matter if the world has marched
    along,
And scorned his slowness as it quickly
    passed;
No matter, if amid the busy throng,
He greets some face, infantile at the last.

His mission ? Well, there is but one,
And if it is a mission he knows it, nay,
To be a happy idler, to lounge and sun,
And dreaming, pass his long-drawn days
    away.

So dreams he on, his happy life to pass
Content, without ambitions painful sighs,
Until the sands run down into the glass;
He   smiles — content — unmoved   and
    and dies

And yet, with all the pity that you feel
For this poor mothling of that flame, the
    world ;
Are you the better for your desperate
    deal,
When you, like him, into infinitude are
    hurled ?

LOVE AND THE BUTTERFLY.

———

I heard a merry voice one day
And glancing at my side,
Fair Love, all breathless, flushed with
　　play,
A butterfly did ride
"Whither away, oh sportive boy?"
I asked, he tossed his head;
Laughing aloud for purest joy,
And past me swiftly sped.

Next day I heard a plaintive cry
And Love crept in my arms;
Weeping he held the butterfly,
Devoid of all its charms.
Sweet words of comfort, whispered I
Into his dainty ears,
But love still hugged the butterfly,
And bathed its wounds with tears.

THE BEE-MAN.

———

We were glancing over the mental photograph album, and commenting on the great lack of dissimilarity in tastes. Nearly every one preferred spring to any other season, with a very few exceptions in favor of autumn. The women loved Mrs. Browning and Longfellow; the men showed decided preferences after Emerson and Macauley. Conceit stuck out when the majority wanted to be themselves and none other, and only two did not want to live in the 19th century. But in one place, in answer to the question, "Whom would you rather be, if not yourself?" the answer was,

"A baby."

"Why would you rather be a baby than any other personage?" queried someone glancing at the writer, who blushed as she replied.

"Because then I might be able to live a better life, I might have better opportunities and better chances for improving them, and it would bring me nearer the 20th century."

"About eight or nine years ago," said the first speaker, "I remember reading a story in a magazine for young folks. It was merely a fairy story, and perhaps was not intended to point a moral, but only to amuse the little ones. It was something on this order : —

Once upon a time, there lived in an out of the way spot an ancient decrepit Bee-man. How old he was no one knew; whence he came, no one could tell : to the memory of the oldest inhabitant he had always lived in his dirty hut, surrounded by myriads of hives, attended always by a swarm of bees. He was good to the bits of children, and always ready with a sweet morsel of honeycomb for them. All his ambitions, sympathies and hopes were centered in his hives; until one day a fairy crept into his hut and whispered :

"You have not always been a common

bee-man. Once you were something else."

" Tell me what I was," he asked eagerly.

" Nay, that I cannot do," replied the fairy,' our queen sent me to tell you this, and if you wished to search for your former self, I am to assist you. You must search the entire valley, and the first thing you meet to which you become violently attached, that is what you formerly were, and I shall give you back your correct form."

So the next morning the Bee-man, strapping his usual hive upon his back, and accompanied by the fairy in the form of a queen bee, set out upon his search throughout the valley. At first he became violently attached to the handsome per-on and fine castle of the Lord of the Realm, but on being kicked out of the lord's domains, his love turned to dislike.

The Bee-man and the fairy travelled far and wide and carefully inspected every thing they met. The very Imp, the Languid young man, the Hippogriffith, the Thousand Tailed Hippotamus, and many other types, until the Bee-man grew weary and was about to give up t e search in disgust.

But suddenly amid all the vast halls of the enchanted domains through which they were wandering, there sounded shrieks and wails, and the inmates were thrown into the greatest confusion by the sight of the hideous hippogriffith dashing through, a million sparks emanating from his great eyes, his barbed tail waving high in the air, and holding in his talons a tiny infant.

Now, as soon as the Bee-man saw this, a great wave of sorrow and pity filled his breast, and he hastily followed the mons-ter, arriving at his cave just in time to see him preparing to devour his prey. Madly dashing his hive of bees in o the hippogriffith's face, and seizing the in-fant while the disturbed and angry bees stung and swarmed, the Bee-man rushed out followed by the Very Imp, the Lan-guid young man and the fairy, and made

his way to the child's mother. Just as
soon as the baby was safely restored,
the Bee-man ruminated thoughtfully
awhile and finally remarked to the fairy:

" Do you know of all the things I have
met so far, I liked the baby best of all,
·so I think I must have been a baby
once!"

" Right you are," assented the fairy,
" I knew it before, but, of course, I
couldn't tell. Now I shall change you
into your former shape, but remember,
you must try to be something better than
a Bee-man."

The Bee-man promised and was instantly changed into a baby. The fairy
inoculated him from harm with a bee-
sting, and gave him to the rescued infant's mother.

Nearly a cycle passed by, and one day
the fairy having business in the valley,
thought she would make inquiries concerning her protege. In her way she
happened to pass a little, low, curious
hut, with many bee hives about it, and

swarms of bees flying in and out. The
fairy, tired as well as curious, peeped in
and discovered an ancient man attending
to the wants of his pets. Upon a closer
inspection, she recognized her infant of
years ago. He had become a bee-man
again!"

———

" It points a pretty little moral," said
the Fatalist, " for it certainly proves that
do what we will, we cannot get away
from our natures. It was inherent in
that man's nature to tend bees. Bee-ing
was the occupation chosen for him by
Fate, and had the beneficent Fairy
changed him a dozen times, he would
ultimately have gone to bee-ing in some
form or other."

The Fatalist was doubtless right, for it
seems as though the inherent things in
our nature must come out. But if we
want to dig deep into the child's story
for metaphysical morals, does it not also
uphold the theory of re-incarnation ? the
ancient bee-man, perhaps is but a type

of humanity growing old, and settled in its mode of living, while the fairy is but thought, whispering into our souls things half dread half pleasant.

There are moments when the consciousness of a former life comes sharply upon us, in swift, lightning flashes, too sudden to be tangible, too dazzling to leave an impress, or mayhap, in troubled dreams that bewilder and confuse with vague remembrances. If only a burst of memory would come upon some mortal, that the tale might be fully told, and these theories established as facts. It would unfold great possibilities of historical lore; of literary life; of religious speculation.

AMID THE ROSES.

There is tropical warmth and languerous
    life
    Where the roses lie
    In a tempting drift
Of pink and red and golden light
Untouched as yet by the pruning knife.
And the still, warm life of the roses fair
    That whisper "Come,"
    With promises
Of sweet caresses, close and pure
Has a thorny whiff in the perfumed air.
There are thorns and love in the roses'
    bed,
    And Satan too
    Must linger there;
So Satan's wiles and the conscience
    stings,
Must now abide—the roses are *dead*.

THE GOODNESS OF ST. ROCQUE
AND OTHER STORIES

The GOODNESS OF ST. ROCQUE

AND OTHER STORIES

By

ALICE DUNBAR

New York: DODD, MEAD AND COMPANY

Mdcccxcix

University Press
John Wilson and Son, Cambridge, U.S.A.

To

My best Comrade

My Husband

CONTENTS

THE GOODNESS OF SAINT ROCQUE

THE GOODNESS OF SAINT ROCQUE

Manuela was tall and slender and graceful, and once you knew her the lithe form could never be mistaken. She walked with the easy spring that comes from a perfectly arched foot. To-day she swept swiftly down Marais Street, casting a quick glance here and there from under her heavy veil as if she feared she was being followed. If you had peered under the veil, you would have seen that Manuela's dark eyes were swollen and discoloured about the lids, as though they had known a sleepless, tearful night.

There had been a picnic the day before, and as merry a crowd of giddy, chattering Creole girls and boys as

ever you could see boarded the ram-
shackle dummy-train that puffed its
way wheezily out wide Elysian Fields
Street, around the lily-covered bayous,
to Milneburg-on-the-Lake.   Now, a
picnic at Milneburg is a thing to be
remembered for ever.   One charters a
rickety-looking, weather-beaten danc-
ing-pavilion, built over the water, and
after storing the children — for your
true Creole never leaves the small folks
at home — and the baskets and mothers
downstairs, the young folks go up-
stairs and dance to the tune of the best
band you ever heard.   For what can
equal the music of a violin, a guitar, a
cornet, and a bass viol to trip the quadrille to at a picnic ?

Then one can fish in the lake and go
bathing under the prim bath-houses,
so severely separated sexually, and go
rowing on the lake in a trim boat, followed by the shrill warnings of anx-

ious mamans. And in the evening one comes home, hat crowned with cool gray Spanish moss, hands burdened with fantastic latanier baskets woven by the brown bayou boys, hand in hand with your dearest one, tired but happy.

At this particular picnic, however, there had been bitterness of spirit. Theophilé was Manuela's own especial property, and Theophilé had proven false. He had not danced a single waltz or quadrille with Manuela, but had deserted her for Claralie, blonde and petite. It was Claralie whom Theophilé had rowed out on the lake; it was Claralie whom Theophilé had gallantly led to dinner; it was Claralie's hat that he wreathed with Spanish moss, and Claralie whom he escorted home after the jolly singing ride in town on the little dummy-train.

Not that Manuela lacked partners or admirers. Dear no! she was too graceful and beautiful for that. There had been more than enough for her. But Manuela loved Theophilé, you see, and no one could take his place. Still, she had tossed her head and let her silvery laughter ring out in the dance, as though she were the happiest of mortals, and had tripped home with Henri, leaning on his arm, and looking up into his eyes as though she adored him.

This morning she showed the traces of a sleepless night and an aching heart as she walked down Marais Street. Across wide St. Rocque Avenue she hastened. " Two blocks to the river and one below —" she repeated to herself breathlessly. Then she stood on the corner gazing about her, until with a final summoning of a desperate courage she dived through a small wicket gate into a garden of weed-choked flowers.

There was a hoarse, rusty little bell on the gate that gave querulous tongue as she pushed it open. The house that sat back in the yard was little and old and weather-beaten. Its one-story frame had once been painted, but that was a memory remote and traditional. A straggling morning-glory strove to conceal its time-ravaged face. The little walk of broken bits of brick was reddened carefully, and the one little step was scrupulously yellow-washed, which denoted that the occupants were cleanly as well as religious.

Manuela's timid knock was answered by a harsh " Entrez."

It was a small sombre room within, with a bare yellow-washed floor and ragged curtains at the little window. In a corner was a diminutive altar draped with threadbare lace. The red glow of the taper lighted a cheap print of St. Joseph and a brazen crucifix. The human element in the room was furnished by a little, wizened yellow woman, who, black-robed, turbaned, and stern, sat before an uncertain table whereon were greasy cards.

Manuela paused, her eyes blinking at the semi-obscurity within. The Wizened One called in croaking tones:

"An' fo' w'y you come here? Assiez-là, ma'amzelle."

Timidly Manuela sat at the table facing the owner of the voice.

" I want," she began faintly; but the Mistress of the Cards understood: she had had much experience. The cards were shuffled in her long grimy talons and stacked before Manuela.

" Now you cut dem in t'ree part, so — un, deux, trois, bièn ! You mek' you' weesh wid all you' heart, bien ! Yaas, I see, I see !"

Breathlessly did Manuela learn that her lover was true, but " dat light gal,

yaas, she mek' nouvena in St. Rocque
fo' hees love."

"I give you one lil' charm, yaas,"
said the Wizened One when the séance
was over, and Manuela, all white and
nervous, leaned back in the rickety
chair. "I give you one lil' charm fo'
to ween him back, yaas. You wear
h'it 'roun' you' wais', an' he come
back. Den you mek prayer at St.
Rocque an' burn can'le. Den you
come back an' tell me, yaas. Cinquante
sous, ma'amzelle. Merci. Good luck
go wid you."

Readjusting her veil, Manuela passed
out the little wicket gate, treading on
air. Again the sun shone, and the
breath of the swamps came as health-
ful sea-breeze unto her nostrils. She
fairly flew in the direction of St.
Rocque.

There were quite a number of
persons entering the white gates of

the cemetery, for this was Friday,
when all those who wish good luck
pray to the saint, and wash their steps
promptly at twelve o'clock with a
wondrous mixture to guard the house.
Manuela bought a candle from the
keeper of the little lodge at the entrance, and pausing one instant by the
great sun-dial to see if the heavens and
the hour were propitious, glided into
the tiny chapel, dim and stifling with
heavy air from myriad wish-candles
blazing on the wide table before the
altar-rail. She said her prayer and
lighting her candle placed it with the
others.

Mon Dieu ! how brightly the sun
seemed to shine now, she thought,
pausing at the door on her way out.
Her small finger-tips, still bedewed with
holy water, rested caressingly on a
gamin's head. The ivy which enfolds
the quaint chapel never seemed so

green; the shrines which serve as the
Way of the Cross never seemed so
artistic; the baby graves, even, seemed
cheerful.

Theophilé called Sunday. Manuela's
heart leaped. He had been spending
his Sundays with Claralie. His stay
was short and he was plainly bored.
But Manuela knelt to thank the good
St. Rocque that night, and fondled the
charm about her slim waist. There
came a box of bonbons during the
week, with a decorative card all roses
and fringe, from Theophilé; but being
a Creole, and therefore superstitiously
careful, and having been reared by a
wise and experienced maman to mistrust
the gifts of a recreant lover, Manuela
quietly thrust bonbons, box, and card
into the kitchen fire, and the Friday
following placed the second candle of
her nouvena in St. Rocque.

Those of Manuela's friends who had

watched with indignation Theophilé
gallantly leading Claralie home from
High Mass on Sundays, gasped with
astonishment when the next Sunday,
with his usual bow, the young man
offered Manuela his arm as the wor-
shippers filed out in step to the
organ's march. Claralie tossed her
head as she crossed herself with holy
water, and the pink in her cheeks was
brighter than usual.

Manuela smiled a bright good-morn-
ing when she met Claralie in St. Rocque
the next Friday. The little blonde
blushed furiously, and Manuela rushed
post-haste to the Wizened One to
confer upon this new issue.

" H'it ees good," said the dame, shak-
ing her turbaned head. " She ees 'fraid,
she will work, mais you' charm, h'it
weel beat her."

And Manuela departed with radiant
eyes.

Theophilé was not at Mass Sunday morning, and murderous glances flashed from Claralie to Manuela before the tinkling of the Host-Bell. Nor did Theophilé call at either house. Two hearts beat furiously at the sound of every passing footstep, and two minds wondered if the other were enjoying the beloved one's smiles. Two pair of eyes, however, blue and black, smiled on others, and their owners laughed and seemed none the less happy. For your Creole girls are proud, and would die rather than let the world see their sorrows.

Monday evening Theophilé, the missing, showed his rather sheepish countenance in Manuela's parlour, and explained that he, with some chosen spirits, had gone for a trip — "over the Lake."

"I did not ask you where you were yesterday," replied the girl, saucily.

Theophilé shrugged his shoulders and changed the conversation.

The next week there was a birthday fête in honour of Louise, Theophilé's young sister. Everyone was bidden, and no one thought of refusing, for Louise was young, and this would be her first party. So, though the night was hot, the dancing went on as merrily as light young feet could make it go. Claralie fluffed her dainty white skirts, and cast mischievous sparkles in the direction of Theophilé, who with the maman and Louise was bravely trying not to look self-conscious. Manuela, tall and calm and proud-looking, in a cool, pale yellow gown was apparently enjoying herself without paying the slightest attention to her young host.

" Have I the pleasure of this dance ?" he asked her finally, in a lull of the music.

She bowed assent, and as if moved

by a common impulse they strolled out of the dancing-room into the cool, quaint garden, where jessamines gave out an overpowering perfume, and a caged mocking-bird complained melodiously to the full moon in the sky.

It must have been an engrossing tête-a-tête, for the call to supper had sounded twice before they heard and hurried into the house. The march had formed with Louise radiantly leading on the arm of papa. Claralie tripped by with Leon. Of course, nothing remained for Theophilé and Manuela to do but to bring up the rear, for which they received much good-natured chaffing.

But when the party reached the dining-room, Theophilé proudly led his partner to the head of the table, at the right hand of maman, and smiled benignly about at the delighted assemblage. Now you know, when a Creole young man places a girl at his mother's right hand at his own table, there is but one conclusion to be deduced therefrom.

If you had asked Manuela, after the wedding was over, how it happened, she would have said nothing, but looked wise.

If you had asked Claralie, she would have laughed and said she always preferred Leon.

If you had asked Theophilé, he would have wondered that you thought he had ever meant more than to tease Manuela.

If you had asked the Wizened One, she would have offered you a charm.

But St. Rocque knows, for he is a good saint, and if you believe in him and are true and good, and make your nouvenas with a clean heart, he will grant your wish.

TONY'S WIFE

TONY'S WIFE

"Gimme fi' cents worth o' candy, please." It was the little Jew girl who spoke, and Tony's wife roused herself from her knitting to rise and count out the multi-hued candy which should go in exchange for the dingy nickel grasped in warm, damp fingers. Three long sticks, carefully wrapped in crispest brown paper, and a half dozen or more of pink candy fish for lagniappe, and the little Jew girl sped away in blissful contentment. Tony's wife resumed her knitting with a stifled sigh until the next customer should come.

A low growl caused her to look up apprehensively. Tony himself stood beetle-browed and huge in the small doorway.

"Get up from there," he muttered, "and open two dozen oysters right away; the Eliots want 'em." His English was unaccented. It was long since he had seen Italy.

She moved meekly behind the counter, and began work on the thick shells. Tony stretched his long neck up the street.

"Mr. Tony, mama wants some charcoal." The very small voice at his feet must have pleased him, for his black brows relaxed into a smile, and he poked the little one's chin with a hard, dirty finger, as he emptied the ridiculously small bucket of charcoal into the child's bucket, and gave a banana for lagniappe.

The crackling of shells went on behind, and a stifled sob arose as a bit of sharp edge cut into the thin, worn fingers that clasped the knife.

"Hurry up there, will you?"

growled the black brows; "the Eliots
are sending for the oysters."

She deftly strained and counted
them, and, after wiping her fingers,
resumed her seat, and took up the endless crochet work, with her usual stifled
sigh.

Tony and his wife had always been
in this same little queer old shop on
Prytania Street, at least to the memory
of the oldest inhabitant in the neighbourhood. When or how they came, or
how they stayed, no one knew ; it was
enough that they were there, like a sort
of ancestral fixture to the street. The
neighbourhood was fine enough to look
down upon these two tumble-down
shops at the corner, kept by Tony
and Mrs. Murphy, the grocer. It was
a semi-fashionable locality, far up-town,
away from the old-time French quarter.
It was the sort of neighbourhood where
millionaires live before their fortunes are

made and fashionable, high-priced private schools flourish, where the small cottages are occupied by aspiring schoolteachers and choir-singers. Such was this locality, and you must admit that it was indeed a condescension to tolerate Tony and Mrs. Murphy.

He was a great, black-bearded, hoarse-voiced, six-foot specimen of Italian humanity, who looked in his little shop and on the prosaic pavement of Prytania Street somewhat as Hercules might seem in a modern drawing-room. You instinctively thought of wild mountain-passes, and the gleaming dirks of bandit contadini in looking at him. What his last name was, no one knew. Someone had maintained once that he had been christened Antonio Malatesta, but that was unauthentic, and as little to be believed as that other wild theory that her name was Mary.

She was meek, pale, little, ugly, and German. Altogether part of his arms and legs would have very decently made another larger than she. Her hair was pale and drawn in sleek, thin tightness away from a pinched, pitiful face, whose dull cold eyes hurt you, because you knew they were trying to mirror sorrow, and could not because of their expressionless quality. No matter what the weather or what her other toilet, she always wore a thin little shawl of dingy brick-dust hue about her shoulders. No matter what the occasion or what the day, she always carried her knitting with her, and seldom ceased the incessant twist, twist of the shining steel among the white cotton meshes. She might put down the needles and lace into the spool-box long enough to open oysters, or wrap up fruit and candy, or count out wood and coal into infinitesimal portions, or do her housework; but the knitting was snatched with avidity at the first spare moment, and the worn, white, blue-marked fingers, half enclosed in kid-glove stalls for protection, would writhe and twist in and out again. Little girls just learning to crochet borrowed their patterns from Tony's wife, and it was considered quite a mark of advancement to have her inspect a bit of lace done by eager, chubby fingers. The ladies in larger houses, whose husbands would be millionaires some day, bought her lace, and gave it to their servants for Christmas presents.

As for Tony, when she was slow in opening his oysters or in cooking his red beans and spaghetti, he roared at her, and prefixed picturesque adjectives to her lace, which made her hide it under her apron with a fearsome look in her dull eyes.

He hated her in a lusty, roaring fashion, as a healthy beefy boy hates a sick cat and torments it to madness. When she displeased him, he beat her, and knocked her frail form on the floor. The children could tell when this had happened. Her eyes would be red, and there would be blue marks on her face and neck. " Poor Mrs. Tony," they would say, and nestle close to her. Tony did not roar at her for petting them, perhaps, because they spent money on the multi-hued candy in glass jars on the shelves.

Her mother appeared upon the scene once, and stayed a short time; but Tony got drunk one day and beat her because she ate too much, and she disappeared soon after. Whence she came and where she departed, no one could tell, not even Mrs. Murphy, the Pauline Pry and Gazette of the block.

Tony had gout, and suffered for

many days in roaring helplessness, the
while his foot, bound and swathed in
many folds of red flannel, lay on the
chair before him. In proportion as his
gout increased and he bawled from
pure physical discomfort, she became
light-hearted, and moved about the
shop with real, brisk cheeriness. He
could not hit her then without such
pain that after one or two trials he
gave up in disgust.

So the dull years had passed, and life
had gone on pretty much the same for
Tony and the German wife and the
shop. The children came on Sunday
evenings to buy the stick candy, and
on week-days for coal and wood. The
servants came to buy oysters for the
larger houses, and to gossip over the
counter about their employers. The
little dry woman knitted, and the big
man moved lazily in and out in his red
flannel shirt, exchanged politics with

the tailor next door through the window, or lounged into Mrs. Murphy's bar and drank fiercely. Some of the children grew up and moved away, and other little girls came to buy candy and eat pink lagniappe fishes, and the shop still thrived.

One day Tony was ill, more than the mummied foot of gout, or the wheeze of asthma; he must keep his bed and send for the doctor.

She clutched his arm when he came, and pulled him into the tiny room.

" Is it — is it anything much, doctor? " she gasped.

Æsculapius shook his head as wisely as the occasion would permit. She followed him out of the room into the shop.

" Do you — will he get well, doctor? "

Æsculapius buttoned up his frock coat, smoothed his shining hat, cleared his throat, then replied oracularly,

"Madam, he is completely burned out inside. Empty as a shell, madam, empty as a shell. He cannot live, for he has nothing to live on."

As the cobblestones rattled under the doctor's equipage rolling leisurely up Prytania Street, Tony's wife sat in her chair and laughed,—laughed with a hearty joyousness that lifted the film from the dull eyes and disclosed a sparkle beneath.

The drear days went by, and Tony lay like a veritable Samson shorn of his strength, for his voice was sunken to a hoarse, sibilant whisper, and his black eyes gazed fiercely from the shock of hair and beard about a white face. Life went on pretty much as before in the shop; the children paused to ask how Mr. Tony was, and even hushed the jingles on their bell hoops as they passed the door. Red-headed Jimmie, Mrs. Murphy's nephew, did the hard

jobs, such as splitting wood and lifting
coal from the bin; and in the intervals
between tending the fallen giant and
waiting on the customers, Tony's wife
sat in her accustomed chair, knitting
fiercely, with an inscrutable smile about
her purple compressed mouth.

Then John came, introducing himself, serpent-wise, into the Eden of her
bosom.

John was Tony's brother, huge and
bluff too, but fair and blond, with the
beauty of Northern Italy. With the
same lack of race pride which Tony
had displayed in selecting his German
spouse, John had taken unto himself
Betty, a daughter of Erin, aggressive,
powerful, and cross-eyed. He turned up
now, having heard of this illness, and
assumed an air of remarkable authority
at once.

A hunted look stole into the dull
eyes, and after John had departed with

blustering directions as to Tony's welfare, she crept to his bedside timidly.

"Tony," she said,—"Tony, you are very sick."

An inarticulate growl was the only response.

"Tony, you ought to see the priest; you must n't go any longer without taking the sacrament."

The growl deepened into words.

"Don't want any priest; you're always after some snivelling old woman's fuss. You and Mrs. Murphy go on with your church; it won't make *you* any better."

She shivered under this parting shot, and crept back into the shop. Still the priest came next day.

She followed him in to the bedside and knelt timidly.

"Tony," she whispered, "here's Father Leblanc."

Tony was too languid to curse out

loud; he only expressed his hate in a
toss of the black beard and shaggy
mane.

"Tony," she said nervously, "won't
you do it now? It won't take long,
and it will be better for you when you
go— Oh, Tony, don't—don't laugh.
Please, Tony, here's the priest."

But the Titan roared aloud: "No;
get out. Think I'm a-going to give
you a chance to grab my money now?
Let me die and go to hell in peace."

Father Leblanc knelt meekly and
prayed, and the woman's weak pleadings
continued, —

"Tony, I've been true and good
and faithful to you. Don't die and
leave me no better than before. Tony,
I do want to be a good woman once,
a real-for-true married woman. Tony,
here's the priest; say yes." And she
wrung her ringless hands.

"You want my money," said Tony,

slowly, "and you sha'n't have it, not a cent; John shall have it."

Father Leblanc shrank away like a fading spectre. He came next day and next day, only to see re-enacted the same piteous scene,—the woman pleading to be made a wife ere death hushed Tony's blasphemies, the man chuckling in pain-racked glee at the prospect of her bereaved misery. Not all the prayers of Father Leblanc nor the wailings of Mrs. Murphy could alter the determination of the will beneath the shock of hair; he gloated in his physical weakness at the tenacious grasp on his mentality.

"Tony," she wailed on the last day, her voice rising to a shriek in its eagerness, "tell them I'm your wife; it'll be the same. Only say it, Tony, before you die!"

He raised his head, and turned stiff eyes and gibbering mouth on her; then, with one chill finger pointing at John, fell back dully and heavily.

They buried him with many honours by the Society of Italia's Sons. John took possession of the shop when they returned home, and found the money hidden in the chimney corner.

As for Tony's wife, since she was not his wife after all, they sent her forth in the world penniless, her worn fingers clutching her bundle of clothes in nervous agitation, as though they regretted the time lost from knitting.

THE FISHERMAN OF PASS CHRISTIAN

THE FISHERMAN OF PASS CHRISTIAN.

THE swift breezes on the beach at Pass Christian meet and conflict as though each strove for the mastery of the air. The land-breeze blows down through the pines, resinous, fragrant, cold, bringing breath-like memories of dim, dark woods shaded by myriad pine-needles. The breeze from the Gulf is warm and soft and languorous, blowing up from the south with its suggestion of tropical warmth and passion. It is strong and masterful, and tossed Annette's hair and whipped her skirts about her in bold disregard for the proprieties.

Arm in arm with Philip, she was strolling slowly down the great pier which extends from the Mexican Gulf

Hotel into the waters of the Sound. There was no moon to-night, but the sky glittered and scintillated with myriad stars, brighter than you can ever see farther North, and the great waves that the Gulf breeze tossed up in restless profusion gleamed with the white fire of phosphorescent flame. The wet sands on the beach glowed white fire; the posts of the pier where the waves had leapt and left a laughing kiss, the sides of the little boats and fish-cars tugging at their ropes, alike showed white and flaming, as though the sea and all it touched were afire.

Annette and Philip paused midway the pier to watch two fishermen casting their nets. With heads bared to the breeze, they stood in clear silhouette against the white background of sea.

" See how he uses his teeth," almost whispered Annette.

Drawing himself up to his full height,

with one end of the huge seine between
his teeth, and the cord in his left hand,
the taller fisherman of the two paused
a half instant, his right arm extended,
grasping the folds of the net. There
was a swishing rush through the air,
and it settled with a sort of sob as it
cut the waters and struck a million
sparkles of fire from the waves. Then,
with backs bending under the strain,
the two men swung on the cord, drawing in the net, laden with glittering
restless fish, which were unceremoni-
ously dumped on the boards to be put
into the fish-car awaiting them.

Philip laughingly picked up a soft,
gleaming jelly-fish, and threatened to
put it on Annette's neck. She screamed,
ran, slipped on the wet boards, and in
another instant would have fallen over
into the water below. The tall fisherman caught her in his arms and set her
on her feet.

"Mademoiselle must be very careful," he said in the softest and most correct French. "The tide is in and the water very rough. It would be very difficult to swim out there to-night."

Annette murmured confused thanks, which were supplemented by Philip's hearty tones. She was silent until they reached the pavilion at the end of the pier. The semi-darkness was unrelieved by lantern or light. The strong wind wafted the strains from a couple of mandolins, a guitar, and a tenor voice stationed in one corner to sundry engrossed couples in sundry other corners. Philip found an untenanted nook and they ensconced themselves therein.

"Do you know there's something mysterious about that fisherman?" said Annette, during a lull in the wind.

"Because he did not let you go over?" inquired Philip.

"No; he spoke correctly, and with the accent that goes only with an excellent education."

Philip shrugged his shoulders. "That's nothing remarkable. If you stay about Pass Christian for any length of time, you'll find more things than perfect French and courtly grace among fishermen to surprise you. These are a wonderful people who live across the Lake."

Annette was lolling in the hammock under the big catalpa-tree some days later, when the gate opened, and Natalie's big sun-bonnet appeared. Natalie herself was discovered blushing in its dainty depths. She was only a little Creole seaside girl, you must know, and very shy of the city demoiselles. Natalie's patois was quite as different from Annette's French as it was from the postmaster's English.

"Mees Annette," she began, peony-

hued all over at her own boldness,
" we will have one lil' hay-ride this
night, and a fish-fry at the end.   Will
you come? "

Annette sprang to her feet in delight.
" Will I come?   Certainly.   How delightful!   You are so good to ask me.
What shall — what time — " But Natalie's pink bonnet had fled precipitately
down the shaded walk.   Annette
laughed joyously as Philip lounged
down the gallery.

" I frightened the child away," she
told him.

You 've never been for a hay-ride
and fish-fry on the shores of the Mississippi Sound, have you?   When the
summer boarders and the Northern
visitors undertake to give one, it is a
comparatively staid affair, where due
regard is had for one's wearing apparel,
and where there are servants to do the
hardest work.   Then it is n't enjoyable

at all. But when the natives, the boys and girls who live there, make up their minds to have fun, you may depend upon its being just the best kind.

This time there were twenty boys and girls, a mamma or so, several papas, and a grizzled fisherman to restrain the ardor of the amateurs. The cart was vast and solid, and two comfortable, sleepy-looking mules constituted the drawing power. There were also tin horns, some guitars, an accordeon, and a quartet of much praised voices. The hay in the bottom of the wagon was freely mixed with pine needles, whose prickiness through your hose was amply compensated for by its delicious fragrance.

After a triumphantly noisy passage down the beach one comes to the stretch of heavy sand that lies between Pass Christian proper and Henderson's

Point. This is a hard pull for the
mules, and the more ambitious riders
get out and walk. Then, after a final
strain through the shifting sands, bravo !
the shell road is reached, and one goes
cheering through the pine-trees to
Henderson's Point.

If ever you go to Pass Christian, you
must have a fish-fry at Henderson's
Point. It is the pine-thicketed, white-
beached peninsula jutting out from the
land, with one side caressed by the
waters of the Sound and the other
purred over by the blue waves of the
Bay of St. Louis. Here is the beginning of the great three-mile trestle
bridge to the town of Bay St. Louis,
and to-night from the beach could be
seen the lights of the villas glittering
across the Bay like myriads of unsleep-
ing eyes.

Here upon a firm stretch of white
sand camped the merry-makers. Soon

a great fire of driftwood and pine
cones tossed its flames defiantly at a
radiant moon in the sky, and the fishers
were casting their nets in the sea. The
more daring of the girls waded bare-
legged in the water, holding pine-
torches, spearing flounders and peering
for soft-shell crabs.

Annette had wandered farther in the
shallow water than the rest. Suddenly
she stumbled against a stone, the torch
dropped and spluttered at her feet.
With a little helpless cry she looked
at the stretch of unfamiliar beach and
water to find herself all alone.

"Pardon me, mademoiselle," said a
voice at her elbow; "you are in distress?"

It was her fisherman, and with a
scarce conscious sigh of relief, Annette
put her hand into the outstretched
one at her side.

"I was looking for soft shells," she

explained, "and lost the crowd, and now my torch is out."

"Where is the crowd?" There was some amusement in the tone, and Annette glanced up quickly, prepared to be thoroughly indignant at this fisherman who dared make fun at her; but there was such a kindly look about his mouth that she was reassured and said meekly,—

"At Henderson's Point."

"You have wandered a half-mile away," he mused, "and have nothing to show for your pains but very wet skirts. If mademoiselle will permit me, I will take her to her friends, but allow me to suggest that mademoiselle will leave the water and walk on the sands."

"But I am barefoot," wailed Annette, "and I am afraid of the fiddlers."

Fiddler crabs, you know, aren't pleasant things to be dangling around

one's bare feet, and they are more
numerous than sand fleas down at
Henderson's Point.

"True," assented the fisherman;
"then we shall have to wade back."

The fishing was over when they
rounded the point and came in sight
of the cheery bonfire with its Rembrandt-
like group, and the air was savoury with
the smell of frying fish and crabs. The
fisherman was not to be tempted by
appeals to stay, but smilingly disappeared down the sands, the red glare
of his torch making a glowing track in
the water.

"Ah, Mees Annette," whispered Natalie, between mouthfuls of a rich croaker,
"you have found a beau in the water."

"And the fisherman of the Pass, too,"
laughed her cousin Ida.

Annette tossed her head, for Philip
had growled audibly.

"Do you know, Philip," cried

Annette a few days after, rudely shak-
ing him from his siesta on the gallery, —
" do you know that I have found my
fisherman's hut ? "

" Hum," was the only response.

" Yes, and it's the quaintest, most
delightful spot imaginable.   Philip, do
come with me and see it."

" Hum."

" Oh, Philip, you are so lazy; do
come with me."

" Yes, but, my dear Annette," pro-
tested Philip, " this is a warm day, and
I am tired."

Still, his curiosity being aroused, he
went grumbling.   It was not a very
long drive, back from the beach across
the   railroad   and   through   the   pine
forest to the bank of a dark, slow-flow-
ing bayou.   The fisherman's hut was
small, two-roomed, whitewashed, pine-
boarded, with the traditional mud
chimney acting as a sort of support to

one of its uneven sides. Within was
a weird assortment of curios from every
uncivilized part of the globe. Also
were there fishing-tackle and guns in
reckless profusion. The fisherman, in
the kitchen of the mud-chimney, was
sardonically waging war with a basket
of little bayou crabs.

"Entrez, mademoiselle et monsieur,"
he said pleasantly, grabbing a vicious
crab by its flippers, and smiling at
its wild attempts to bite. "You see
I am busy, but make yourself at
home."

"Well, how on earth —" began
Philip.

"Sh — sh —" whispered Annette.
"I was driving out in the woods this
morning, and stumbled on the hut.
He asked me in, but I came right over
after you."

The fisherman, having succeeded in
getting the last crab in the kettle of

boiling water, came forward smiling and began to explain the curios.

"Then you have not always lived at Pass Christian," said Philip.

"Mais non, monsieur, I am spending a summer here."

"And he spends his winters, doubtless, selling fish in the French market," spitefully soliloquised Philip.

The fisherman was looking unutterable things into Annette's eyes, and, it seemed to Philip, taking an unconscionably long time explaining the use of an East Indian stiletto.

"Oh, wouldn't it be delightful!" came from Annette at last.

"What?" asked Philip.

"Why, Monsieur LeConte says he'll take six of us out in his catboat tomorrow for a fishing-trip on the Gulf."

"Hum," drily.

"And I'll get Natalie and her cousins."

"Yes," still more drily.

Annette chattered on, entirely oblivious of the strainedness of the men's adieux, and still chattered as they drove through the pines.

"I did not know that you were going to take fishermen and marchands into the bosom of your social set when you came here," growled Philip, at last.

"But, Cousin Phil, can't you see he is a gentleman? The fact that he makes no excuses or protestations is a proof."

"You are a fool," was the polite response.

Still, at six o'clock next morning, there was a little crowd of seven upon the pier, laughing and chatting at the little "Virginie" dipping her bows in the water and flapping her sails in the brisk wind. Natalie's pink bonnet blushed in the early sunshine, and Natalie's

mamma, comely and portly, did chaper-
onage duty.   It was not long before
the sails gave swell into the breeze and
the little boat scurried to the Sound.
Past the lighthouse on its gawky iron
stalls, she flew, and now rounded the
white sands of Cat Island.

" Bravo, the Gulf!" sang a voice on
the lookout.   The little boat dipped,
halted an instant, then rushed fast into
the blue Gulf waters.

" We will anchor here," said the host,
" have luncheon, and fish."

Philip could not exactly understand
why the fisherman should sit so close
to Annette and whisper so much into
her ears.   He chafed at her acting the
part of hostess, and was possessed of a
murderous desire to throw the pink
sun-bonnet and its owner into the sea,
when Natalie whispered audibly to one
of her cousins that " Mees Annette act
nice wit' her lovare."

The sun was banking up flaming
pillars of rose and gold in the west
when the little " Virginie " rounded Cat
Island on her way home, and the quick
Southern twilight was fast dying into
darkness when she was tied up to the
pier and the merry-makers sprang off
with baskets of fish.   Annette had distinguished herself by catching one small
shark, and had immediately ceased to
fish and devoted her attention to her
fisherman and his line.   Philip had
angled fiercely, landing trout, croakers,
sheepshead, snappers in bewildering
luck.   He had broken each hopeless
captive's neck savagely, as though they
were personal enemies.   He did not
look happy as they landed, though
pæans of praise were being sung in his
honour.

As the days passed on, " the fisherman of the Pass " began to dance
attendance on Annette.   What had

seemed a joke became serious. Aunt
Nina, urged by Philip, remonstrated,
and even the mamma of the pink sun-
bonnet began to look grave. It was
all very well for a city demoiselle to
talk with a fisherman and accept favours
at his hands, provided that the city
demoiselle understood that a vast and
bridgeless gulf stretched between her
and the fisherman. But when the
demoiselle forgot the gulf and the
fisherman refused to recognise it, why,
it was time to take matters in hand.

To all of Aunt Nina's remonstran-
ces, Philip's growlings, and the averted
glances of her companions, Annette
was deaf. " You are narrow-minded,"
she said laughingly. " I am interested
in Monsieur LeConte simply as a
study. He is entertaining; he talks
well of his travels, and as for refusing to
recognise the difference between us, why,
he never dreamed of such a thing."

Suddenly a peremptory summons home from Annette's father put an end to the fears of Philip. Annette pouted, but papa must be obeyed. She blamed Philip and Aunt Nina for telling tales, but Aunt Nina was uncommunicative, and Philip too obviously cheerful to derive much satisfaction from.

That night she walked with the fisherman hand in hand on the sands. The wind from the pines bore the scarcely recognisable, subtle freshness of early autumn, and the waters had a hint of dying summer in their sob on the beach.

"You will remember," said the fisher-man, "that I have told you nothing about myself."

"Yes," murmured Annette.

"And you will keep your promises to me?"

"Yes."

"Let me hear you repeat them again."

" I promise you that I will not forget you. I promise you that I will never speak of you to anyone until I see you again. I promise that I will then clasp your hand wherever you may be."

" And mademoiselle will not be discouraged, but will continue her studies?"

" Yes."

It was all very romantic, by the waves of the Sound, under a harvest moon, that seemed all sympathy for these two, despite the fact that it was probably looking down upon hundreds of other equally romantic couples. Annette went to bed with glowing cheeks, and a heart whose pulsations would have caused a physician to prescribe unlimited digitalis.

It was still hot in New Orleans when she returned home, and it seemed hard to go immediately to work   But if one is going to be an opera-singer some

day and capture the world with one's
voice, there is nothing to do but to
study, study, sing, practise, even though
one's throat be parched, one's head a
great ache, and one's heart a nest of
discouragement and sadness at what
seems the uselessness of it all. Annette
had now a new incentive to work; the
fisherman had once praised her voice
when she hummed a barcarole on the
sands, and he had insisted that there was
power in its rich notes. Though the
fisherman had showed no cause why he
should be accepted as a musical critic,
Annette had somehow respected his
judgment and been accordingly elated.

It was the night of the opening of
the opera. There was the usual crush,
the glitter and confusing radiance of
the brilliant audience. Annette, with
papa, Aunt Nina, and Philip, was late
reaching her box. The curtain was

up, and "La Juive" was pouring forth defiance at her angry persecutors. Annette listened breathlessly. In fancy, she too was ringing her voice out to an applauding house. Her head unconsciously beat time to the music, and one hand half held her cloak from her bare shoulders.

Then Eleazar appeared, and the house rose at the end of his song. Encores it gave, and bravos and cheers. He bowed calmly, swept his eyes over the tiers until they found Annette, where they rested in a half-smile of recognition.

"Philip," gasped Annette, nervously raising her glasses, "my fisherman!"

"Yes, an opera-singer is better than a marchand," drawled Philip.

The curtain fell on the first act. The house was won by the new tenor; it called and recalled him before the curtain. Clearly he had sung his way into the hearts of his audience at once.

"Papa, Aunt Nina," said Annette, "you must come behind the scenes with me. I want you to meet him. He is delightful. You must come."

Philip was bending ostentatiously over the girl in the next box. Papa and Aunt Nina consented to be dragged behind the scenes. Annette was well known, for, in hopes of some day being an occupant of one of the dressing-rooms, she had made friends with everyone connected with the opera.

Eleazar received them, still wearing his brown garb and patriarchal beard.

"How you deceived me!" she laughed, when the greetings and introductions were over.

"I came to America early," he smiled back at her, "and thought I'd try a little incognito at the Pass. I was not well, you see.   It has been of great benefit to me."

"I kept my promise," she said in a lower tone.

"Thank you; that also has helped me."

Annette's teacher began to note a wonderful improvement in his pupil's voice.   Never did a girl study so hard or practise so faithfully.   It was truly wonderful.   Now and then Annette would say to papa as if to reassure herself, —

"And when Monsieur Cherbart says I am ready to go to Paris, I may go, papa?"

And papa would say a "Certainly" that would send her back to the piano with renewed ardour.

As for Monsieur LeConte, he was the idol of New Orleans.   Seldom had there been a tenor who had sung himself so completely into the very hearts

of a populace. When he was billed,
the opera displayed " Standing Room "
signs, no matter what the other attractions in the city might be. Sometimes
Monsieur LeConte delighted small
audiences in Annette's parlour, when
the hostess was in a perfect flutter of
happiness. Not often, you know, for
the leading tenor was in great demand
at the homes of society queens.

" Do you know," said Annette, petulantly, one evening, " I wish for the old
days at Pass Christian."

" So do I," he answered tenderly ;
" will you repeat them with me next
summer ? "

" If I only could ! " she gasped.

Still she might have been happy, had
it not been for Madame Dubeau, —
Madame Dubeau, the flute-voiced leading soprano, who wore the single dainty
curl on her forehead, and thrilled her
audiences oftentimes more completely

than the fisherman.   Madame Dubeau
was La Juive to his Eleazar, Leonore
to his Manfred, Elsa to his Lohengrin,
Aida to his Rhadames, Marguerite to
his Faust; in brief, Madame Dubeau
was his opposite.   She caressed him as
Mignon, pleaded with him as Michaela,
died for him in " Les Huguenots," broke
her heart for love of him in " La Favorite."   How could he help but love
her, Annette asked herself, how could
he?   Madame Dubeau was beautiful
and gifted and charming.

Once she whispered her fears to him
when there was the meagrest bit of an
opportunity. He laughed. "You don't
understand, little one," he said tenderly; " the relations of professional
people to each other are peculiar. After
you go to Paris, you will know."

Still, New Orleans had built up its
romance, and gossiped accordingly.

" Have you heard the news? " whis-

pered Lola to Annette, leaning from
her box at the opera one night. The
curtain had just gone up on " Hero-
dias," and for some reason or other,
the audience applauded with more
warmth than usual. There was a
noticeable number of good-humoured,
benignant smiles on the faces of the
applauders.

" No," answered Annette, breathlessly,— " no, indeed, Lola ; I am going
to Paris next week. I am so delighted
I can't stop to think."

" Yes, that is excellent," said Lola,
" but all New Orleans is smiling at
the romance. Monsieur LeConte and
Madame Dubeau were quietly married
last night, but it leaked out this afternoon. See all the applause she's
receiving ! "

Annette leaned back in her chair,
very white and still. Her box was
empty after the first act, and a quiet

little tired voice that was almost too faint to be heard in the carriage on the way home, said —

"Papa, I don't think I care to go to Paris, after all."

M'SIEU FORTIER'S VIOLIN

M'SIEU FORTIER'S VIOLIN

SLOWLY, one by one, the lights in the French Opera go out, until there is but a single glimmer of pale yellow flickering in the great dark space, a few moments ago all a-glitter with jewels and the radiance of womanhood and a-clash with music. Darkness now, and silence, and a great haunted hush over all, save for the distant cheery voice of a stage hand humming a bar of the opera.

The glimmer of gas makes a halo about the bowed white head of a little old man putting his violin carefully away in its case with aged, trembling, nervous fingers. Old M'sieu Fortier was the last one out every night.

Outside the air was murky, foggy. Gas and electricity were but faint splotches of light on the thick curtain of fog and mist.   Around the opera was a mighty bustle of carriages and drivers and footmen, with a car gaining headway in the street now and then, a howling of names and numbers, the laughter and small talk of cloaked society stepping slowly to its carriages, and the more bourgeoisie vocalisation of the foot passengers who streamed along and hummed little bits of music.   The fog's denseness was confusing, too, and at one moment it seemed that the little narrow street would become inextricably choked and remain so until some mighty engine would blow the crowd into atoms.   It had been a crowded night.   From around Toulouse Street, where led the entrance to the troisièmes, from the grand stairway, from the entrance to the quatrièmes, the human stream poured into the street, nearly all with a song on their lips.

M'sieu Fortier stood at the corner, blinking at the beautiful ladies in their carriages. He exchanged a hearty salutation with the saloon-keeper at the corner, then, tenderly carrying his violin case, he trudged down Bourbon Street, a little old, bent, withered figure, with shoulders shrugged up to keep warm, as though the faded brown overcoat were not thick enough.

Down on Bayou Road, not so far from Claiborne Street, was a house, little and old and queer, but quite large enough to hold M'sieu Fortier, a wrinkled dame, and a white cat. He was home but little, for on nearly every day there were rehearsals; then on Tuesday, Thursday, and Saturday nights, and twice Sundays there were performances, so Ma'am Jeanne and the white cat kept house almost always alone. Then, when M'sieu Fortier was at home, why, it was practice, practice all

the day, and smoke, snore, sleep at night.
Altogether it was not very exhilarating.

M'sieu Fortier had played first violin
in the orchestra ever since — well, no
one remembered his not playing there.
Sometimes there would come breaks
in the seasons, and for a year the great
building would be dark and silent.
Then M'sieu Fortier would do jobs of
playing here and there, one night for this
ball, another night for that soirée dan-
sante, and in the day, work at his trade,
— that of a cigar-maker.   But now for
seven years there had been no break in
the season, and the little old violinist
was happy.   There is nothing sweeter
than a regular job and good music to
play, music into which one can put
some soul, some expression, and which
one must study to understand.   Dance
music, of the frivolous, frothy kind
deemed essential to soirées, is trivial,
easy, uninteresting.

So M'sieu Fortier, Ma'am Jeanne, and the white cat lived a peaceful, uneventful existence out on Bayou Road. When the opera season was over in February, M'sieu went back to cigar-making, and the white cat purred none the less contentedly.

It had been a benefit to-night for the leading tenor, and he had chosen "Roland à Ronceveaux," a favourite this season, for his farewell. And, mon Dieu, mused the little M'sieu, but how his voice had rung out bell-like, piercing above the chorus of the first act ! Encore after encore was given, and the bravos of the troisièmes were enough to stir the most sluggish of pulses.

> " Superbes Pyrenées
> Qui dressez dans le ciel,
> Vos cimes couronnées
> D'un hiver éternelle,
> Pour nous livrer passage
> Ouvrez vos larges flancs,
> Faîtes taire l'orage,
> Voici, venir les Francs ! "

M'sieu quickened his pace down Bourbon Street as he sang the chorus to himself in a thin old voice, and then, before he could see in the thick fog, he had run into two young men.

" I — I — beg your pardon, — messieurs," he stammered.

" Most certainly," was the careless response; then the speaker, taking a second glance at the object of the rencontre, cried joyfully:

" Oh, M'sieu Fortier, is it you? Why, you are so happy, singing your love sonnet to your lady's eyebrow, that you did n't see a thing but the moon, did you? And who is the fair one who should clog your senses so? "

There was a deprecating shrug from the little man.

" Ma foi, but monsieur must know fo' sho', dat I am too old for love songs ! "

" I know nothing save that I want

that violin of yours.   When is it to be
mine, M'sieu Fortier?"

"Nevare, nevare!" exclaimed M'sieu,
gripping on as tightly to the case as if
he feared it might be wrenched from
him.   "Me a lovere, and to sell mon
violon!   Ah, so ver' foolish !"

"Martel," said the first speaker to
his companion as they moved on up
town, "I wish you knew that little
Frenchman.   He's a unique specimen.
He has the most exquisite violin I've
seen in years; beautiful and mellow as
a genuine Cremona, and he can make
the music leap, sing, laugh, sob, skip,
wail, anything you like from under his
bow when he wishes.   It's something
wonderful.   We are good friends.
Picked him up in my French-town
rambles.   I've been trying to buy that
instrument since —"

"To throw it aside a week later?"
lazily inquired Martel.   "You are like

the rest of these nineteenth-century vandals, you can see nothing pictur-esque that you do not wish to deface for a souvenir; you cannot even let simple happiness alone, but must needs destroy it in a vain attempt to make it your own or parade it as an advertisement."

As for M'sieu Fortier, he went right on with his song and turned into Bayou Road, his shoulders still shrugged high as though he were cold, and into the quaint little house, where Ma'am Jeanne and the white cat, who always waited up for him at nights, were both nodding over the fire.

It was not long after this that the opera closed, and M'sieu went back to his old out-of-season job. But some-how he did not do as well this spring and summer as always. There is a cer-tain amount of cunning and finesse required to roll a cigar just so, that

M'sieu seemed to be losing, whether from age or deterioration it was hard to tell. Nevertheless, there was just about half as much money coming in as formerly, and the quaint little pucker between M'sieu's eyebrows which served for a frown came oftener and stayed longer than ever before.

"Minesse," he said one day to the white cat, — he told all his troubles to her; it was of no use to talk to Ma'am Jeanne, she was too deaf to understand, — "Minesse, we are gettin' po'. You' père git h'old, an' hees han's dey go no mo' rapidement, an' dere be no mo' soirées dese day. Minesse, eef la saison don' hurry up, we shall eat ver' lil' meat."

And Minesse curled her tail and purred.

Before the summer had fairly begun, strange rumours began to float about in musical circles. M. Maugé would no longer manage the opera, but it would be turned into the hands of Americans, a syndicate. Bah! These English-speaking people could do nothing unless there was a trust, a syndicate, a company immense and dishonest. It was going to be a guarantee business, with a strictly financial basis. But worse than all this, the new manager, who was now in France, would not only procure the artists, but a new orchestra, a new leader. M'sieu Fortier grew apprehensive at this, for he knew what the loss of his place would mean to him.

September and October came, and the papers were filled with accounts of the new artists from France and of the new orchestra leader too. He was described as a most talented, progressive, energetic young man. M'sieu Fortier's heart sank at the word "progressive." He was anything but that.

The New Orleans Creole blood flowed
too sluggishly in his old veins.

November came; the opera reopened.
M'sieu Fortier was not re-engaged.

"Minesse," he said with a catch in
his voice that strongly resembled a sob,
"Minesse, we mus' go hongry sometime. Ah, mon pauvre violon! Ah,
mon Dieu, dey put us h'out, an' dey
will not have us. Nev' min', we will
sing anyhow." And drawing his bow
across the strings, he sang in his thin,
quavering voice, "Salut demeure, chaste
et pure."

It is strange what a peculiar power
of fascination former haunts have for
the human mind. The criminal, after
he has fled from justice, steals back
and skulks about the scene of his
crime; the employee thrown from work
hangs about the place of his former
industry; the schoolboy, truant or ex-
pelled, peeps in at the school-gate and

taunts the good boys within.   M'sieu
Fortier was no exception.   Night after
night of the performances he climbed
the stairs of the opera and sat, an atten-
tive listener to the orchestra, with one
ear inclined to the stage, and a quizzi-
cal expression on his wrinkled face.
Then he would go home, and pat
Minesse, and fondle the violin.

"Ah, Minesse, dose new player!
Not one bit can dey play.   Such tones,
Minesse, such tones !   All the time
portemento, oh, so ver' bad !   Ah, mon
chere violon, we can play."   And he
would play and sing a romance, and
smile tenderly to himself.

At first it used to be into the deux-
ièmes that M'sieu Fortier went, into
the front seats.   But soon they were
too expensive, and after all, one could
hear just as well in the fourth row as in
the first.   After a while even the rear
row of the deuxiemes was too costly,

and the little musician wended his way
with the plebeians around on Toulouse
Street, and climbed the long, tedious
flight of stairs into the troisièmes. It
makes no difference to be one row
higher. It was more to the liking, after
all. One felt more at home up here
among the people. If one was thirsty,
one could drink a glass of wine or beer
being passed about by the libretto boys,
and the music sounded just as well.

But it happened one night that
M'sieu could not even afford to climb
the Toulouse Street stairs. To be sure,
there was yet another gallery, the quatrièmes, where the peanut boys went for a
dime, but M'sieu could not get down to
that yet. So he stayed outside until all
the beautiful women in their warm
wraps, a bright-hued chattering throng,
came down the grand staircase to their
carriages.

It was on one of these nights that

Courcey and Martel found him shivering at the corner.

"Hello, M'sieu Fortier," cried Courcey, "are you ready to let me have that violin yet?"

"For shame!" interrupted Martel.

"Fifty dollars, you know," continued Courcey, taking no heed of his friend's interpolation.

M'sieu Fortier made a courtly bow. "Eef Monsieur will call at my 'ouse on de morrow, he may have mon violon," he said huskily; then turned abruptly on his heel, and went down Bourbon Street, his shoulders drawn high as though he were cold.

When Courcey and Martel entered the gate of the little house on Bayou Road the next day, there floated out to their ears a wordless song thrilling from the violin, a song that told more than speech or tears or gestures could have done of the utter sorrow and desolation of the little old man. They walked softly up the short red brick walk and tapped at the door. Within, M'sieu Fortier was caressing the violin, with silent tears streaming down his wrinkled gray face.

There was not much said on either side. Courcey came away with the instrument, leaving the money behind, while Martel grumbled at the essentially sordid, mercenary spirit of the world. M'sieu Fortier turned back into the room, after bowing his visitors out with old-time French courtliness, and turning to the sleepy white cat, said with a dry sob :

"Minesse, dere's only me an' you now."

About six days later, Courcey's morning dreams were disturbed by the announcement of a visitor. Hastily doing a toilet, he descended the stairs to find M'sieu Fortier nervously pacing the hall floor.

"I come fo' bring back you' money, yaas. I cannot sleep, I cannot eat, I only cry, and t'ink, and weesh fo' mon violon; and Minesse, an' de ol' woman too, dey mope an' look bad too, all for mon violon. I try fo' to use dat money, but eet burn an' sting lak blood money. I feel lak' I done sol' my child. I cannot go at l'opera no mo', I t'ink of mon violon. I starve befo' I live widout. My heart, he is broke, I die for mon violon."

Courcey left the room and returned with the instrument.

"M'sieu Fortier," he said, bowing low, as he handed the case to the little man, "take your violin; it was a whim with me, a passion with you. And as for the money, why, keep that too; it was worth a hundred dollars to have possessed such an instrument even for six days."

BY THE BAYOU ST. JOHN

BY THE BAYOU ST. JOHN

The Bayou St. John slowly makes its dark-hued way through reeds and rushes, high banks and flat slopes, until it casts itself into the turbulent bosom of Lake Pontchartrain. It is dark, like the passionate women of Egypt; placid, like their broad brows; deep, silent, like their souls. Within its bosom are hidden romances and stories, such as were sung by minstrels of old. From the source to the mouth is not far distant, visibly speaking, but in the life of the bayou a hundred heart-miles could scarce measure it. Just where it winds about the northwest of the city are some of its most beautiful bits, orange groves on one side, and quaint old Spanish gardens on the other.

Who cares that the bridges are modern, and that here and there pert boat-houses rear their prim heads ? It is the bayou, even though it be invaded with the ruthless vandalism of the improving idea, and can a boat-house kill the beauty of a moss-grown centurion of an oak with a history as old as the city ? Can an iron bridge with tarantula piers detract from the song of a mocking-bird in a fragrant orange grove? We know that farther out, past the Confederate Soldiers' Home, — that rose-embowered, rambling place of gray-coated, white-haired old men with broken hearts for a lost cause, — it flows, unimpeded by the faintest conception of man, and we love it all the more that, like the Priestess of Isis, it is calm-browed, even in indignity.

To its banks at the end of Moss Street, one day there came a man and a maiden. They were both tall and lithe and slender, with the agility of youth and fire. He was the final concentration of the essence of Spanish passion filtered into an American frame; she, a repressed Southern exotic, trying to fit itself into the niches of a modern civilisation. Truly, a fitting couple to seek the bayou banks.

They climbed the levee that stretched a feeble check to waters that seldom rise, and on the other side of the embankment, at the brink of the river, she sat on a log, and impatiently pulled off the little cap she wore. The skies were gray, heavy, overcast, with an occasional wind-rift in the clouds that only revealed new depths of grayness behind; the tideless waters murmured a faint ripple against the logs and jutting beams of the breakwater, and were answered by the crescendo wail of the dried reeds on the other bank, — reeds that rustled and moaned among themselves for the golden days of summer sunshine.

He stood up, his dark form a slender silhouette against the sky; she looked upward from her log, and their eyes met with an exquisite shock of recognising understanding; dark eyes into dark eyes, Iberian fire into Iberian fire, soul unto soul: it was enough. He sat down and took her into his arms, and in the eerie murmur of the storm coming they talked of the future.

"And then I hope to go to Italy or France. It is only there, beneath those far Southern skies, that I could ever hope to attain to anything that the soul within me says I can. I have wasted so much time in the mere struggle for bread, while the powers of a higher calling have clamoured for recognition and expression. I will go some day and redeem myself."

She was silent a moment, watching

with half-closed lids a dejected-looking
hunter on the other bank, and a lean
dog who trailed through the reeds
behind him with drooping tail. Then
she asked:

"And I — what will become of me?"

"You, Athanasia? There is a great
future before you, little woman, and I
and my love can only mar it. Try to
forget me and go your way. I am only
the epitome of unhappiness and ill-
success."

But she laughed and would have
none of it.

Will you ever forget that day, Athanasia? How the little gamins, Creole
throughout, came half shyly near the
log, fishing, and exchanging furtive
whispers and half-concealed glances at
the silent couple. Their angling was
rewarded only by a little black water-
moccasin that wriggled and forked its
venomous red tongue in an attempt to

exercise its death-dealing prerogative. This Athanasia insisted must go back into its native black waters, and paid the price the boys asked that it might enjoy its freedom. The gamins laughed and chattered in their soft patois; the Don smiled tenderly upon Athanasia, and she durst not look at the reeds as she talked, lest their crescendo sadness yield a foreboding. Just then a wee girl appeared, clad in a multi-hued garment, evidently a sister to the small fishermen. Her keen black eyes set in a dusky face glanced sharply and suspiciously at the group as she clambered over the wet embankment, and it seemed the drizzling mist grew colder, the sobbing wind more pronounced in its prophetic wail. Athanasia rose suddenly. " Let us go," she said; " the eternal feminine has spoiled it all."

The bayou flows as calmly, as darkly, as full of hidden passions as ever. On a night years after, the moon was shining upon it with a silvery tenderness that seemed brighter, more caressingly lingering than anywhere within the old city. Behind, there rose the spires and towers; before, only the reeds, green now, and soft in their rustlings and whisperings for the future. False reeds! They tell themselves of their happiness to be, and it all ends in dry stalks and drizzling skies. The mocking-bird in the fragrant orange grove sends out his night song, and blends it with the cricket's chirp, as the blossoms of orange and magnolia mingle their perfume with the earthy smell of a summer rain just blown over. Perfect in its stillness, absolute in its beauty, tenderly healing in its suggestion of peace, the night in its clear-lighted, cloudless sweetness enfolds Athanasia, as she stands on the levee and gazes down at the old log, now almost hidden in the luxuriant grass.

" It was the eternal feminine that spoiled our dream that day as it spoiled the after life, was it not ? "

But the Bayou St. John did not answer.   It merely gathered into its silent bosom another broken-hearted romance, and flowed dispassionately on its way.

WHEN THE BAYOU OVERFLOWS

WHEN THE BAYOU
OVERFLOWS

WHEN the sun goes down behind the great oaks along the Bayou Teche near Franklin, it throws red needles of light into the dark woods, and leaves a great glow on the still bayou. Ma'am Mouton paused at her gate and cast a contemplative look at the red sky.

"Hit will rain to-morrow, sho'. I mus' git in my t'ings."

Ma'am Mouton's remark must have been addressed to herself or to the lean dog, for no one else was visible. She moved briskly about the yard, taking things from the line, when Louisette's voice called cheerily:

"Ah, Ma'am Mouton, can I help?"

Louisette was petite and plump and

black-haired.   Louisette's eyes danced,
and her lips were red and tempting.
Ma'am Mouton's face relaxed as the
small brown hands relieved hers of
their burden.

"Sylves', has he come yet?" asked
the red mouth.

"Mais non, ma chère," said Ma'am
Mouton, sadly, " I can' tell fo' w'y he
no come home soon dese day. Ah
me, I feel lak' somet'ing goin' happen.
He so strange."

Even as she spoke a quick nervous
step was heard crunching up the brick
walk. Sylves' paused an instant without the kitchen door, his face turned
to the setting sun. He was tall and
slim and agile; a true 'cajan.

" Bon jour, Louisette," he laughed
" Eh, maman ! "

" Ah, my son, you are ver' late."

Sylves' frowned, but said nothing.
It was a silent supper that followed.

Louisette was sad, Ma'am Mouton sighed now and then, Sylves' was constrained.

"Maman," he said at length, "I am goin' away."

Ma'am Mouton dropped her fork and stared at him with unseeing eyes; then, as she comprehended his remark, she put her hand out to him with a pitiful gesture.

"Sylves'!" cried Louisette, springing to her feet.

"Maman, don't, don't!" he said weakly; then gathering strength from the silence, he burst forth:

"Yaas, I'm goin' away to work. I'm tired of dis, jus' dig, dig, work in de fiel', nothin' to see but de cloud, de tree, de bayou. I don't lak' New Orleans; it too near here, dere no mo' money dere. I go up fo' Mardi Gras, an' de same people, de same strit'. I'm goin' to Chicago!"

"Sylves'!" screamed both women at once.

Chicago! That vast, far-off city that seemed in another world. Chicago! A name to conjure with for wickedness.

"W'y, yaas," continued Sylves', "lots of boys I know dere. Henri an' Joseph Lascaud an' Arthur, dey write me what money dey mek' in cigar. I can mek' a livin' too. I can mek' fine cigar. See how I do in New Orleans in de winter."

"Oh, Sylves'," wailed Louisette, "den you 'll forget me!"

"Non, non, ma chère," he answered tenderly. "I will come back when the bayou overflows again, an' maman an' Louisette will have fine present."

Ma'am Mouton had bowed her head on her hands, and was rocking to and fro in an agony of dry-eyed misery.

Sylves' went to her side and knelt. "Maman," he said softly, "maman, you mus' not cry. All de boys go 'way, an' I will come back reech, an' you won't have fo' to work no mo'."

But Ma'am Mouton was inconsolable.

It was even as Sylves' had said. In the summer-time the boys of the Bayou Teche would work in the field or in the town of Franklin, hack-driving and doing odd jobs. When winter came, there was a general exodus to New Orleans, a hundred miles away, where work was to be had as cigarmakers. There is money, plenty of it, in cigar-making, if one can get in the right place. Of late, however, there had been a general slackness of the trade. Last winter oftentimes Sylves' had walked the streets out of work. Many were the Creole boys who had gone to Chicago to earn a living, for the cigar-making trade flourishes there wonderfully. Friends of Sylves' had gone, and written home glowing accounts of the money to be had almost for the asking.   When one's blood leaps for new scenes, new adventures, and one needs money, what is the use of frittering away time alternately between the Bayou Teche and New Orleans? Sylves' had brooded all summer, and now that September had come, he was determined to go.

Louisette, the orphan, the girl-lover, whom everyone in Franklin knew would some day be Ma'am Mouton's daughter-in-law, wept and pleaded in vain.   Sylves' kissed her quivering lips.

" Ma chère," he would say, " t'ink, I will bring you one fine diamon' ring, nex' spring, when de bayou overflows again."

Louisette would fain be content with this promise.   As for Ma'am Mouton, she seemed to have grown ages older.

Her Sylves' was going from her; Sylves',
whose trips to New Orleans had been
a yearly source of heart-break, was
going far away for months to that
mistily wicked city, a thousand miles
away.

October came, and Sylves' had gone.
Ma'am Mouton had kept up bravely
until the last, when with one final cry
she extended her arms to the pitiless
train bearing him northward. Then
she and Louisette went home drearily,
the one leaning upon the other.

Ah, that was a great day when the
first letter came from Chicago! Louisette came running in breathlessly from
the post-office, and together they read
it again and again. Chicago was such
a wonderful city, said Sylves'. Why,
it was always like New Orleans at
Mardi Gras with the people. He had
seen Joseph Lascaud, and he had a
place to work promised him. He was

well, but he wanted, oh, so much, to see maman and Louisette. But then, he could wait.

Was ever such a wonderful letter? Louisette sat for an hour afterwards building gorgeous air-castles, while Ma'am Mouton fingered the paper and murmured prayers to the Virgin for Sylves'. When the bayou overflowed again? That would be in April. Then Louisette caught herself looking critically at her slender brown fingers, and blushed furiously, though Ma'am Mouton could not see her in the gathering twilight.

Next week there was another letter, even more wonderful than the first. Sylves' had found work. He was making cigars, and was earning two dollars a day. Such wages! Ma'am Mouton and Louisette began to plan pretty things for the brown cottage on the Teche.

That was a pleasant winter, after all. True, there was no Sylves', but then he was always in New Orleans for a few months any way. There were his letters, full of wondrous tales of the great queer city, where cars went by ropes underground, and where there was no Mardi Gras and the people did not mind Lent. Now and then there would be a present, a keepsake for Louisette, and some money for maman. They would plan improvements for the cottage, and Louisette began to do sewing and dainty crochet, which she would hide with a blush if anyone hinted at a trousseau.

It was March now, and Spring-time. The bayou began to sweep down between its banks less sluggishly than before; it was rising, and soon would spread over its tiny levees. The doors could be left open now, though the trees were not yet green; but then down here the trees do not swell and bud slowly and tease you for weeks with promises of greenness. Dear no, they simply look mysterious, and their twigs shake against each other and tell secrets of the leaves that will soon be born. Then one morning you awake, and lo, it is a green world! The boughs have suddenly clothed them- selves all in a wondrous garment, and you feel the blood run riot in your veins out of pure sympathy.

One day in March, it was warm and sweet. Underfoot were violets, and wee white star flowers peering through the baby-grass. The sky was blue, with flecks of white clouds reflecting themselves in the brown bayou. Louisette tripped up the red brick walk with the Chicago letter in her hand, and paused a minute at the door to look upon the leaping waters, her eyes dancing.

"I know the bayou must be ready
to overflow," went the letter in the
carefully phrased French that the
brothers taught at the parochial school,
"and I am glad, for I want to see the
dear maman and my Louisette. I am
not so well, and Monsieur le docteur
says it is well for me to go to the
South again."

Monsieur le docteur! Sylves' not
well! The thought struck a chill to
the hearts of Ma'am Mouton and
Louisette, but not for long. Of
course, Sylves' was not well, he needed
some of maman's tisanes. Then he was
homesick; it was to be expected.

At last the great day came, Sylves'
would be home. The brown waters of
the bayou had spread until they were
seemingly trying to rival the Mississippi in width. The little house was
scrubbed and cleaned until it shone
again. Louisette had looked her

dainty little dress over and over to be
sure that there was not a flaw to be
found wherein Sylves' could compare
her unfavourably to the stylish Chicago
girls.

The train rumbled in on the platform, and two pair of eyes opened wide
for the first glimpse of Sylves'. The
porter, all officiousness and brass
buttons, bustled up to Ma'am Mouton.

"This is Mrs. Mouton?" he inquired deferentially.

Ma'am Mouton nodded, her heart
sinking. "Where is Sylves'?"

"He is here, madam."

There appeared Joseph Lascaud,
then some men bearing Something.
Louisette put her hands up to her
eyes to hide the sight, but Ma'am
Mouton was rigid.

"It was too cold for him," Joseph
was saying to almost deaf ears, "and
he took the consumption. He thought

he could get well when he come home.
He talk all the way down about the
bayou, and about you and Louisette.
Just three hours ago he had a bad
hemorrhage, and he died from weakness. Just three hours ago. He said
he wanted to get home and give Louisette her diamond ring, when the
bayou overflowed."

MR. BAPTISTE

MR. BAPTISTE

He might have had another name; we never knew. Some one had christened him Mr. Baptiste long ago in the dim past, and it sufficed. No one had ever been known who had the temerity to ask him for another cognomen, for though he was a mild-mannered little man, he had an uncomfortable way of shutting up oyster-wise and looking disagreeable when approached concerning his personal history.

He was small: most Creole men are small when they are old. It is strange, but a fact. It must be that age withers them sooner and more effectually than those of un-Latinised extraction. Mr. Baptiste was, furthermore, very much wrinkled and lame. Like the Son of

Man, he had nowhere to lay his head,
save when some kindly family made
room for him in a garret or a barn.
He subsisted by doing odd jobs, white-
washing, cleaning yards, doing errands,
and the like.

The little old man was a frequenter of
the levee. Never a day passed that his
quaint little figure was not seen moving
up and down about the ships. Chiefly
did he haunt the Texas and Pacific
warehouses and the landing-place of the
Morgan-line steamships. This seemed
like madness, for these spots are almost
the busiest on the levee, and the rough
seamen and 'longshoremen have least
time to be bothered with small weak
folks. Still there was method in the
madness of Mr. Baptiste. The Morgan
steamships, as every one knows, ply
between New Orleans and Central and
South American ports, doing the major
part of the fruit trade; and many were

the baskets of forgotten fruit that Mr. Baptiste took away with him unmolested. Sometimes, you know, bananas and mangoes and oranges and citrons will half spoil, particularly if it has been a bad voyage over the stormy Gulf, and the officers of the ships will give away stacks of fruit, too good to go into the river, too bad to sell to the fruit-dealers.

You could see Mr. Baptiste trudging up the street with his quaint one-sided walk, bearing his dilapidated basket on one shoulder, a nondescript head-cover pulled over his eyes, whistling cheerily. Then he would slip in at the back door of one of his clients with a brisk, —

"Ah, bonjour, madame. Now here ees jus' a lil' bit fruit, some bananas. Perhaps madame would cook some for Mr. Baptiste?"

And madame, who understood and knew his ways, would fry him some of the bananas, and set it before him, a

tempting dish, with a bit of madame's
bread and meat and coffee thrown in
for lagniappe; and Mr. Baptiste would
depart, filled and contented, leaving the
load of fruit behind as madame's pay.
Thus did he eat, and his clients were
many, and never too tired or too cross
to cook his meals and get their pay in
baskets of fruit.

One day he slipped in at Madame
Garcia's kitchen door with such a woe-
begone air, and slid a small sack of
nearly ripe plantains on the table with
such a misery-laden sigh, that madame,
who was fat and excitable, threw up
both hands and cried out:

"Mon Dieu, Mistare Baptiste, fo'
w'y you look lak dat? What ees de
mattare?"

For answer, Mr. Baptiste shook
his head gloomily and sighed again.
Madame Garcia moved heavily about
the kitchen, putting the plantains in

a cool spot and punctuating her footsteps with sundry " Mon Dieux" and " Misères."

" Dose cotton!" ejaculated Mr. Baptiste, at last.

"Ah, mon Dieu ! " groaned Madame Garcia, rolling her eyes heavenwards.

" Hit will drive de fruit away ! " he continued.

" Misère! " said Madame Garcia.

" Hit will."

" Oui, oui," said Madame Garcia. She had carefully inspected the plantains, and seeing that they were good and wholesome, was inclined to agree with anything Mr. Baptiste said.

He grew excited. "Yaas, dose cotton-yardmans, dose 'longsho'mans, dey go out on one strik'. Dey t'row down dey tool an' say dey work no mo' wid niggers. Les veseaux, dey lay in de river, no work, no cargo, yaas. Den de fruit ship, dey can' mak' lan', de

mans, dey t'reaten an' say t'ings. Dey
mak' big fight, yaas. Dere no mo'
work on de levee, lak dat. Ever'body
jus' walk roun' an' say cuss word,
yaas ! ' ''

"Oh, mon Dieu, mon Dieu!" groaned
Madame Garcia, rocking her guinea-
blue-clad self to and fro.

Mr. Baptiste picked up his nondescript head-cover and walked out
through the brick-reddened alley, talking excitedly to himself. Madame
Garcia called after him to know if he
did not want his luncheon, but he shook
his head and passed on.

Down on the levee it was even as
Mr. Baptiste had said. The 'longshoremen, the cotton-yardmen, and the
stevedores had gone out on a strike.
The levee lay hot and unsheltered under the glare of a noonday sun. The
turgid Mississippi scarce seemed to
flow, but gave forth a brazen gleam

from its yellow bosom. Great vessels lay against the wharf, silent and un-populated. Excited groups of men clustered here and there among bales of uncompressed cotton, lying about in disorderly profusion. Cargoes of mo-lasses and sugar gave out a sticky sweet smell, and now and then the fierce rays of the sun would kindle tiny blazes in the cotton and splinter-mixed dust underfoot.

Mr. Baptiste wandered in and out among the groups of men, exchanging a friendly salutation here and there. He looked the picture of woe-begone misery.

"Hello, Mr. Baptiste," cried a big, brawny Irishman, "sure an' you look, as if you was about to be hanged."

"Ah, mon Dieu," said Mr. Baptiste, "dose fruit ship be ruined fo' dees strik'."

"Damn the fruit!" cheerily replied

the Irishman, artistically disposing of a mouthful of tobacco juice. "It ain't the fruit we care about, it's the cotton."

"Hear! hear!" cried a dozen lusty comrades.

Mr. Baptiste shook his head and moved sorrowfully away.

"Hey, by howly St. Patrick, here's that little fruit-eater!" called the centre of another group of strikers perched on cotton-bales.

"Hello! Where—" began a second; but the leader suddenly held up his hand for silence, and the men listened eagerly.

It might not have been a sound, for the levee lay quiet and the mules on the cotton-drays dozed languidly, their ears pitched at varying acute angles. But the practised ears of the men heard a familiar sound stealing up over the heated stillness.

"Oh—ho—ho—humph—humph

— humph — ho — ho — ho — oh — o
— o — humph ! ''

Then the faint rattle of chains, and
the steady thump of a machine
pounding.

If ever you go on the levee you'll
know that sound, the rhythmic song
of the stevedores heaving cotton-bales,
and the steady thump, thump, of the
machine compressing them within the
hold of the ship.

Finnegan, the leader, who had held
up his hand for silence, uttered an
oath.

" Scabs !   Men, come on ! ''

There was no need for a further in-
vitation.   The men rose in sullen
wrath and went down the levee, the
crowd gathering in numbers as it
passed along.   Mr. Baptiste followed
in its wake, now and then sighing a
mournful protest which was lost in the
roar of the men.

"Scabs!" Finnegan had said; and the word was passed along, until it seemed that the half of the second District knew and had risen to investigate.

"Oh — ho — ho — humph — humph — humph — oh — ho — ho — oh — o — o — humph!"

The rhythmic chorus sounded nearer, and the cause manifested itself when the curve of the levee above the French Market was passed. There rose a White Star steamer, insolently settling itself to the water as each consignment of cotton bales was compressed into her hold.

"Niggers!" roared Finnegan wrathily.

"Niggers! niggers! Kill'em, scabs!" chorused the crowd.

With muscles standing out like cables through their blue cotton shirts, and sweat rolling from glossy black skins, the Negro stevedores were at work steadily labouring at the cotton, with the rhythmic song swinging its cadence in the hot air. The roar of the crowd caused the men to look up with momentary apprehension, but at the overseer's reassuring word they bent back to work.

Finnegan was a Titan. With livid face and bursting veins he ran into the street facing the French Market, and uprooted a huge block of paving stone. Staggering under its weight, he rushed back to the ship, and with one mighty effort hurled it into the hold.

The delicate poles of the costly machine tottered in the air, then fell forward with a crash as the whole iron framework in the hold collapsed.

" Damn ye," shouted Finnegan, " now yez can pack yer cotton ! "

The crowd's cheers at this changed to howls, as the Negroes, infuriated at their loss, for those costly machines belong to the labourers and not to the ship-owners, turned upon the mob and began to throw brickbats, pieces of iron, chunks of wood, anything that came to hand. It was pandemonium turned loose over a turgid stream, with a malarial sun to heat the passions to fever point.

Mr. Baptiste had taken refuge behind a bread-stall on the outside of the market. He had taken off his cap, and was weakly cheering the Negroes on.

"Bravo! cheered Mr. Baptiste.

"Will yez look at that damned fruit-eatin' Frinchman!" howled McMahon. "Cheerin' the niggers, are you?" and he let fly a brickbat in the direction of the bread-stall.

"Oh, mon Dieu, mon Dieu!" wailed the bread-woman.

Mr. Baptiste lay very still, with a great ugly gash in his wrinkled brown temple. Fishmen and vegetable marchands gathered around him in a quick, sympathetic mass. The individual, the concrete bit of helpless humanity, had more interest for them than the vast, vague fighting mob beyond.

The noon-hour pealed from the brazen throats of many bells, and the numerous hoarse whistles of the steam-boats called the unheeded luncheon-time to the levee workers. The war waged furiously, and groans of the wounded mingled with curses and roars from the combatants.

"Killed instantly," said the surgeon, carefully lifting Mr. Baptiste into the ambulance.

Tramp, tramp, tramp, sounded the militia steadily marching down Decatur Street.

"Whist! do yez hear!" shouted Finnegan; and the conflict had ceased ere the yellow river could reflect the sun from the polished bayonets.

You remember, of course, how long

the strike lasted, and how many battles were fought and lives lost before the final adjustment of affairs. It was a fearsome war, and many forgot afterwards whose was the first life lost in the struggle,—poor little Mr. Baptiste's, whose body lay at the Morgue unclaimed for days before it was finally dropped unnamed into Potter's Field.

A CARNIVAL JANGLE

A CARNIVAL JANGLE

THERE is a merry jangle of bells in the air, an all-pervading sense of jester's noise, and the flaunting vividness of royal colours. The streets swarm with humanity, — humanity in all shapes, manners, forms, laughing, pushing, jostling, crowding, a mass of men and women and children, as varied and assorted in their several individual peculiarities as ever a crowd that gathered in one locality since the days of Babel.

It is Carnival in New Orleans; a brilliant Tuesday in February, when the very air gives forth an ozone intensely exhilarating, making one long to cut capers. The buildings are a blazing mass of royal purple and golden yellow, national flags, bunting, and decorations that laugh in the glint of the Midas sun. The streets are a crush of jesters and maskers, Jim Crows and clowns, ballet girls and Mephistos, Indians and monkeys; of wild and sudden flashes of music, of glittering pageants and comic ones, of befeathered and belled horses; a dream of colour and melody and fantasy gone wild in an effervescent bubble of beauty that shifts and changes and passes kaleidoscope-like before the bewildered eye.

A bevy of bright-eyed girls and boys of that uncertain age that hovers between childhood and maturity, were moving down Canal Street when there was a sudden jostle with another crowd meeting them. For a minute there was a deafening clamour of shouts and laughter, cracking of the whips, which all maskers carry, a jingle and clatter of carnival bells, and the masked and unmasked extricated themselves and moved from each other's paths. But in the confusion a tall Prince of Darkness had whispered to one of the girls in the unmasked crowd: "You'd better come with us, Flo; you're wasting time in that tame gang. Slip off, they'll never miss you; we'll get you a rig, and show you what life is."

And so it happened, when a half-hour passed, and the bright-eyed bevy missed Flo and couldn't find her, wisely giving up the search at last, she, the quietest and most bashful of the lot, was being initiated into the mysteries of "what life is."

Down Bourbon Street and on Toulouse and St. Peter Streets there are quaint little old-world places where one may be disguised effectually for a tiny consideration. Thither, guided by the shapely Mephisto and guarded by the team of jockeys and ballet girls, tripped Flo. Into one of the lowest-ceiled, dingiest, and most ancient-looking of these shops they stepped.

"A disguise for the demoiselle," announced Mephisto to the woman who met them. She was small and wizened and old, with yellow, flabby jaws, a neck like the throat of an alligator, and straight, white hair that stood from her head uncannily stiff.

"But the demoiselle wishes to appear a boy, un petit garçon?" she inquired, gazing eagerly at Flo's long, slender frame. Her voice was old and thin, like the high quavering of an imperfect tuning-fork, and her eyes were sharp as talons in their grasping glance.

"Mademoiselle does not wish such a costume," gruffly responded Mephisto.

"Ma foi, there is no other," said the ancient, shrugging her shoulders. "But one is left now; mademoiselle would make a fine troubadour."

"Flo," said Mephisto, "it's a dare-devil scheme, try it; no one will ever know it but us, and we'll die before we tell. Besides, we must; it's late, and you couldn't find your crowd."

And that was why you might have seen a Mephisto and a slender trouba-dour of lovely form, with mandolin flung across his shoulder, followed by a bevy of jockeys and ballet girls, laughing and singing as they swept down Rampart Street.

When the flash and glare and bril-liancy of Canal Street have palled upon the tired eye, when it is yet too soon to go home to such a prosaic thing as dinner, and one still wishes for novelty, then it is wise to go into the lower dis-tricts. There is fantasy and fancy and grotesqueness run wild in the costum-ing and the behaviour of the maskers. Such dances and whoops and leaps as these hideous Indians and devils do in-

dulge in ; such wild curvetings and long
walks ! In the open squares, where
whole groups do congregate, it is wonderfully amusing. Then, too, there is
a ball in every available hall, a delirious
ball, where one may dance all day for
ten cents; dance and grow mad for joy,
and never know who were your companions, and be yourself unknown.
And in the exhilaration of the day, one
walks miles and miles, and dances and
skips, and the fatigue is never felt.

In Washington Square, away down
where Royal Street empties its stream of
children great and small into the broad
channel of Elysian Fields Avenue, there
was a perfect Indian pow-wow. With a
little imagination one might have willed
away the vision of the surrounding
houses, and fancied one's self again in
the forest, where the natives were holding a sacred riot. The square was
filled with spectators, masked and un-

masked.   It was amusing to watch
these mimic Red-men, they seemed so
fierce and earnest.

Suddenly one chief touched another
on the elbow.   " See that Mephisto
and troubadour over there ? " he whispered huskily.

" Yes ; who are they ? "

" I don't know the devil," responded
the other, quietly, " but I 'd know that
other form anywhere.   It 's Leon, see ?
I know those white hands like a woman's
and that restless head.   Ha ! "

" But there may be a mistake."

" No.   I 'd know that one anywhere ;
I feel it is he.   I 'll pay him now.   Ah,
sweetheart, you 've waited long, but
you shall feast now ! "   He was caressing something long and lithe and glittering beneath his blanket.

In a masked dance it is easy to give
a death-blow between the shoulders.
Two crowds meet and laugh and shout

and mingle almost inextricably, and if a shriek of pain should arise, it is not noticed in the din, and when they part, if one should stagger and fall bleeding to the ground, can any one tell who has given the blow? There is nothing but an unknown stiletto on the ground, the crowd has dispersed, and masks tell no tales anyway. There is murder, but by whom? for what? *Quien sabe?*

And that is how it happened on Carnival night, in the last mad moments of Rex's reign, a broken-hearted mother sat gazing wide-eyed and mute at a horrible something that lay across the bed. Outside the long sweet march music of many bands floated in as if in mockery, and the flash of rockets and Bengal lights illumined the dead, white face of the girl troubadour.

LITTLE MISS SOPHIE

LITTLE MISS SOPHIE

When Miss Sophie knew consciousness again, the long, faint, swelling
notes of the organ were dying away in
distant echoes through the great arches
of the silent church, and she was alone,
crouching in a little, forsaken black
heap at the altar of the Virgin. The
twinkling tapers shone pityingly upon
her, the beneficent smile of the white-
robed Madonna seemed to whisper
comfort. A long gust of chill air swept
up the aisles, and Miss Sophie shivered
not from cold, but from nervousness.

But darkness was falling, and soon
the lights would be lowered, and the
great massive doors would be closed; so,
gathering her thin little cape about her
frail shoulders, Miss Sophie hurried

out, and along the brilliant noisy streets
home.

It was a wretched, lonely little room,
where the cracks let the boisterous
wind whistle through, and the smoky,
grimy walls looked cheerless and unhomelike. A miserable little room in a
miserable little cottage in one of the
squalid streets of the Third District
that nature and the city fathers seemed
to have forgotten.

As bare and comfortless as the
room was Miss Sophie's life. She
rented these four walls from an unkempt little Creole woman, whose
progeny seemed like the promised
offspring of Abraham. She scarcely
kept the flickering life in her pale
little body by the unceasing toil of a
pair of bony hands, stitching, stitching,
ceaselessly, wearingly, on the bands and
pockets of trousers. It was her bread,
this monotonous, unending work; and

though whole days and nights constant labour brought but the most meagre recompense, it was her only hope of life.

She sat before the little charcoal brazier and warmed her transparent, needle-pricked fingers, thinking meanwhile of the strange events of the day. She had been up town to carry the great, black bundle of coarse pants and vests to the factory and to receive her small pittance, and on the way home stopped in at the Jesuit Church to say her little prayer at the altar of the calm white Virgin. There had been a wondrous burst of music from the great organ as she knelt there, an overpowering perfume of many flowers, the glittering dazzle of many lights, and the dainty frou-frou made by the silken skirts of wedding guests. So Miss Sophie stayed to the wedding; for what feminine heart, be it ever so old and seared, does not delight in one? And why

should not a poor little Creole old
maid be interested too?

Then the wedding party had filed
in solemnly, to the rolling, swelling
tones of the organ. Important-looking groomsmen; dainty, fluffy, white-
robed maids; stately, satin-robed, illusion-veiled bride, and happy groom.
She leaned forward to catch a better
glimpse of their faces. "Ah!"—

Those near the Virgin's altar who
heard a faint sigh and rustle on the
steps glanced curiously as they saw a
slight black-robed figure clutch the
railing and lean her head against it.
Miss Sophie had fainted.

"I must have been hungry," she
mused over the charcoal fire in her
little room, "I must have been hungry;"
and she smiled a wan smile, and busied
herself getting her evening meal of coffee
and bread and ham.

If one were given to pity, the first

thought that would rush to one's lips at sight of Miss Sophie would have been, "Poor little woman!" She had come among the bareness and sordidness of this neighbourhood five years ago, robed in crape, and crying with great sobs that seemed to shake the vitality out of her. Perfectly silent, too, she was about her former life; but for all that, Michel, the quartee grocer at the corner, and Madame Laurent, who kept the rabbé shop opposite, had fixed it all up between them, of her sad history and past glories. Not that they knew; but then Michel must invent something when the neighbours came to him as their fountain-head of wisdom.

One morning little Miss Sophie opened wide her dingy windows to catch the early freshness of the autumn wind as it whistled through the yellow-leafed trees. It was one of those calm, blue-misted, balmy, November days

that New Orleans can have when all
the rest of the country is fur-wrapped.
Miss Sophie pulled her machine to the
window, where the sweet, damp wind
could whisk among her black locks.

Whirr, whirr, went the machine, tick-
ing fast and lightly over the belts of
the rough jeans pants. Whirr, whirr,
yes, and Miss Sophie was actually
humming a tune! She felt strangely
light to-day.

"Ma foi," muttered Michel, strolling
across the street to where Madame
Laurent sat sewing behind the counter
on blue and brown-checked aprons,
"but the little ma'amselle sings. Perhaps she recollects."

"Perhaps," muttered the rabbé
woman.

But little Miss Sophie felt restless.
A strange impulse seemed drawing her
up town, and the machine seemed to
run slow, slow, before it would stitch

all of the endless number of jeans belts.
Her fingers trembled with nervous haste
as she pinned up the unwieldy black
bundle of finished work, and her feet
fairly tripped over each other in their
eagerness to get to Claiborne Street,
where she could board the up-town car.
There was a feverish desire to go somewhere, a sense of elation, a foolish
happiness that brought a faint echo of
colour into her pinched cheeks. She
wondered why.

No one noticed her in the car.   Passengers on the Claiborne line are too
much accustomed to frail little black-
robed women with big, black bundles;
it is one of the city's most pitiful sights.
She leaned her head out of the window to catch a glimpse of the oleanders
on Bayou Road, when her attention
was caught by a conversation in the
car.

"Yes, it's too bad for Neale, and

lately married too," said the elder man. "I can't see what he is to do."

Neale! She pricked up her ears. That was the name of the groom in the Jesuit Church.

"How did it happen?" languidly inquired the younger. He was a stranger, evidently; a stranger with a high regard for the faultlessness of male attire.

"Well, the firm failed first; he didn't mind that much, he was so sure of his uncle's inheritance repairing his lost fortunes; but suddenly this difficulty of identification springs up, and he is literally on the verge of ruin."

"Won't some of you fellows who've known him all your lives do to identify him?"

"Gracious man, we've tried; but the absurd old will expressly stipulates that he shall be known only by a certain quaint Roman ring, and unless he has it, no identification, no fortune. He has given the ring away, and that settles it."

"Well, you're all chumps. Why doesn't he get the ring from the owner?"

"Easily said; but — it seems that Neale had some little Creole love-affair some years ago, and gave this ring to his dusky-eyed fiancée. You know how Neale is with his love-affairs, went off and forgot the girl in a month. It seems, however, she took it to heart, — so much so that he's ashamed to try to find her or the ring."

Miss Sophie heard no more as she gazed out into the dusty grass. There were tears in her eyes, hot blinding ones that wouldn't drop for pride, but stayed and scalded. She knew the story, with all its embellishment of heartaches. She knew the ring, too. She remembered the day she had kissed and wept and fondled it, until it seemed her heart must burst under its load of grief before she took it to the pawn-broker's that another might be eased before the end came, — that other her father. The little " Creole love affair" of Neale's had not always been poor and old and jaded-looking; but reverses must come, even Neale knew that, so the ring was at the Mont de Piété. Still he must have it, it was his; it would save him from disgrace and suffering and from bringing the white-gowned bride into sorrow. He must have it; but how?

There it was still at the pawn-broker's; no one would have such an odd jewel, and the ticket was home in the bureau drawer. Well, he must have it; she might starve in the attempt. Such a thing as going to him and telling him that he might redeem it was an impossibility. That good, straight-backed, stiff-necked Creole blood would have

risen in all its strength and choked her.
No; as a present had the quaint Roman
circlet been placed upon her finger, as
a present should it be returned.

The bumping car rode slowly, and
the hot thoughts beat heavily in her
poor little head.   He must have the
ring; but how — the ring — the Roman
ring — the white-robed bride starving
— she was going mad — ah yes — the
church.

There it was, right in the busiest,
most bustling part of the town, its
fresco and bronze and iron quaintly
suggestive of mediæval times.   Within,
all was cool and dim and restful, with
the faintest whiff of lingering incense
rising and pervading the gray arches.
Yes, the Virgin would know and have
pity ; the sweet, white-robed Virgin at
the pretty flower-decked altar, or the
one away up in the niche, far above the
golden dome where the Host was.

Titiche, the busybody of the house, noticed that Miss Sophie's bundle was larger than usual that afternoon. " Ah, poor woman!" sighed Titiche's mother, " she would be rich for Christmas."

The bundle grew larger each day, and Miss Sophie grew smaller. The damp, cold rain and mist closed the white-curtained window, but always there behind the sewing-machine drooped and bobbed the little black-robed figure. Whirr, whirr went the wheels, and the coarse jeans pants piled in great heaps at her side. The Claiborne Street car saw her oftener than before, and the sweet white Virgin in the flowered niche above the gold-domed altar smiled at the little supplicant almost every day.

" Ma foi," said the slatternly land-lady to Madame Laurent and Michel one day, " I no see how she live ! Eat ? Nothin', nothin', almos', and las' night when it was so cold and foggy, eh ?   I

hav' to mek him build fire.   She mos'
freeze."

Whereupon the rumour spread that
Miss Sophie was starving herself to
death to get some luckless relative out
of jail for Christmas; a rumour which
enveloped her scraggy little figure with
a kind of halo to the neighbours when
she appeared on the streets.

November had merged into December, and the little pile of coins was yet
far from the sum needed.   Dear God!
how the money did have to go!   The
rent and the groceries and the coal,
though, to be sure, she used a precious
bit of that.   Would all the work and
saving and skimping do good?   Maybe, yes, maybe by Christmas.

Christmas Eve on Royal Street is no
place for a weakling, for the shouts and
carousals of the roisterers will strike
fear into the bravest ones.   Yet amid
the cries and yells, the deafening blow

of horns and tin whistles, and the
really dangerous fusillade of fireworks, a
little figure hurried along, one hand
clutching tightly the battered hat that
the rude merry-makers had torn off,
the other grasping under the thin black
cape a worn little pocketbook.

Into the Mont de Piété she ran
breathless, eager. The ticket ? Here,
worn, crumpled. The ring ? It was
not gone ? No, thank Heaven ! It
was a joy well worth her toil, she
thought, to have it again.

Had Titiche not been shooting crackers on the banquette instead of peering
into the crack, as was his wont, his big,
round black eyes would have grown
saucer-wide to see little Miss Sophie
kiss and fondle a ring, an ugly clumsy
band of gold.

"Ah, dear ring," she murmured,
"once you were his, and you shall be
his again. You shall be on his finger,

and perhaps touch his heart. Dear ring, ma chère petite de ma cœur, chérie de ma cœur. Je t'aime, je t'aime, oui, oui. You are his; you were mine once too. To-night, just one night, I'll keep you — then — to-morrow, you shall go where you can save him."

The loud whistles and horns of the little ones rose on the balmy air next morning. No one would doubt it was Christmas Day, even if doors and windows were open wide to let in cool air. Why, there was Christmas even in the very look of the mules on the poky cars; there was Christmas noise in the streets, and Christmas toys and Christmas odours, savoury ones that made the nose wrinkle approvingly, issuing from the kitchen. Michel and Madame Laurent smiled greetings across the street at each other, and the salutation from a passer-by recalled the many-progenied landlady to herself.

"Miss Sophie, well, po' soul, not ver' much Chris'mas for her. Mais, I'll jus' call him in fo' to spen' the day with me. Eet'll cheer her a bit."

It was so clean and orderly within the poor little room. Not a speck of dust or a litter of any kind on the quaint little old-time high bureau, unless you might except a sheet of paper lying loose with something written on it. Titiche had evidently inherited his prying propensities, for the landlady turned it over and read,—

Louis,— Here is the ring. I return it to you. I heard you needed it. I hope it comes not too late.   Sophie.

"The ring, where?" muttered the landlady. There it was, clasped between her fingers on her bosom,— a bosom white and cold, under a cold happy face. Christmas had indeed dawned for Miss Sophie.

SISTER JOSEPHA

SISTER JOSEPHA

SISTER JOSEPHA told her beads mechanically, her fingers numb with the accustomed exercise. The little organ creaked a dismal " O Salutaris," and she still knelt on the floor, her white-bonneted head nodding suspiciously. The Mother Superior gave a sharp glance at the tired figure ; then, as a sudden lurch forward brought the little sister back to consciousness, Mother's eyes relaxed into a genuine smile.

The bell tolled the end of vespers, and the sombre-robed nuns filed out of the chapel to go about their evening duties. Little Sister Josepha's work was to attend to the household lamps, but there must have been as much oil spilled upon the table to-night as was

put in the vessels. The small brown
hands trembled so that most of the
wicks were trimmed with points at one
corner which caused them to smoke
that night.

"Oh, cher Seigneur," she sighed,
giving an impatient polish to a refractory chimney, "it is wicked and sinful,
I know, but I am so tired. I can't be
happy and sing any more. It does n't
seem right for le bon Dieu to have me
all cooped up here with nothing to see
but stray visitors, and always the same
old work, teaching those mean little
girls to sew, and washing and filling
the same old lamps. Pah!" And
she polished the chimney with a sudden vigorous jerk which threatened
destruction.

They were rebellious prayers that
the red mouth murmured that night,
and a restless figure that tossed on the
hard dormitory bed. Sister Dominica

called from her couch to know if Sister
Josepha were ill.

"No," was the somewhat short response; then a muttered, "Why can't
they let me alone for a minute? That
pale-eyed Sister Dominica never sleeps;
that's why she is so ugly."

About fifteen years before this night
some one had brought to the orphan
asylum connected with this convent, du
Sacré Cœur, a round, dimpled bit of
three-year-old humanity, who regarded
the world from a pair of gravely twinkling black eyes, and only took a chubby
thumb out of a rosy mouth long enough
to answer in monosyllabic French. It
was a child without an identity; there
was but one name that any one seemed
to know, and that, too, was vague,—
Camille.

She grew up with the rest of the
waifs; scraps of French and American
civilization thrown together to develop

a seemingly inconsistent miniature world. Mademoiselle Camille was a queen among them, a pretty little tyrant who ruled the children and dominated the more timid sisters in charge.

One day an awakening came. When she was fifteen, and almost fully ripenèd into a glorious tropical beauty of the type that matures early, some visitors to the convent were fascinated by her and asked the Mother Superior to give the girl into their keeping.

Camille fled like a frightened fawn into the yard, and was only unearthed with some difficulty from behind a group of palms. Sulky and pouting, she was led into the parlour, picking at her blue pinafore like a spoiled infant.

"The lady and gentleman wish you to go home with them, Camille," said the Mother Superior, in the language of the convent. Her voice was kind and gentle apparently; but the child, accus-

tomed to its various inflections, detected
a steely ring behind its softness, like the
proverbial iron hand in the velvet glove.

" You must understand, madame,"
continued Mother, in stilted English,
" that we never force children from us.
We are ever glad to place them in comfortable — how you say that ? — quar-
ters — maisons — homes — bien ! But
we will not make them go if they do
not wish."

Camille stole a glance at her would-
be guardians, and decided instantly, impulsively, finally. The woman suited
her; but the man ! It was doubtless
intuition of the quick, vivacious sort
which belonged to her blood that served
her. Untutored in worldly knowledge,
she could not divine the meaning of the
pronounced leers and admiration of her
physical charms which gleamed in the
man's face, but she knew it made her
feel creepy, and stoutly refused to go.

Next day Camille was summoned from a task to the Mother Superior's parlour. The other girls gazed with envy upon her as she dashed down the courtyard with impetuous movement. Camille, they decided crossly, received too much notice. It was Camille this, Camille that; she was pretty, it was to be expected. Even Father Ray lingered longer in his blessing when his hands pressed her silky black hair.

As she entered the parlour, a strange chill swept over the girl. The room was not an unaccustomed one, for she had swept it many times, but to-day the stiff black chairs, the dismal crucifixes, the gleaming whiteness of the walls, even the cheap lithograph of the Madonna which Camille had always regarded as a perfect specimen of art, seemed cold and mean.

"Camille, ma chère," said Mother, "I am extremely displeased with you.

Why did you not wish to go with
Monsieur and Madame Lafayé yesterday ?"

The girl uncrossed her hands from
her bosom, and spread them out in a
deprecating gesture.

" Mais, ma mère, I was afraid."

Mother's face grew stern. " No foolishness now," she exclaimed.

" It is not foolishness, ma mère; I
could not help it, but that man looked
at me so funny, I felt all cold chills
down my back. Oh, dear Mother, I
love the convent and the sisters so, I
just want to stay and be a sister too,
may I ? "

And thus it was that Camille took
the white veil at sixteen years. Now
that the period of novitiate was over, it
was just beginning to dawn upon her
that she had made a mistake.

" Maybe it would have been better
had I gone with the funny-looking lady

and gentleman," she mused bitterly one
night. "Oh, Seigneur, I'm so tired and
impatient; it's so dull here, and, dear
God, I'm so young."

There was no help for it. One must
arise in the morning, and help in the
refectory with the stupid Sister Francesca, and go about one's duties with a
prayerful mien, and not even let a sigh
escape when one's head ached with the
eternal telling of beads.

A great fête day was coming, and
an atmosphere of preparation and mild
excitement pervaded the brown walls
of the convent like a delicate aroma.
The old Cathedral around the corner
had stood a hundred years, and all the
city was rising to do honour to its
age and time-softened beauty. There
would be a service, oh, but such a one!
with two Cardinals, and Archbishops
and Bishops, and all the accompanying
glitter of soldiers and orchestras. The

little sisters of the Convent du Sacré
Cœur clasped their hands in anticipation of the holy joy. Sister Josepha
curled her lip, she was so tired of
churchly pleasures.

The day came, a gold and blue spring
day, when the air hung heavy with
the scent of roses and magnolias, and
the sunbeams fairly laughed as they
kissed the houses. The old Cathedral
stood gray and solemn, and the flowers
in Jackson Square smiled cheery birthday greetings across the way. The
crowd around the door surged and
pressed and pushed in its eagerness to
get within. Ribbons stretched across
the banquette were of no avail to repress it, and important ushers with
cardinal colours could do little more.

The Sacred Heart sisters filed slowly
in at the side door, creating a momentary flutter as they paced reverently to
their seats, guarding the blue-bonneted

orphans. Sister Josepha, determined to
see as much of the world as she could,
kept her big black eyes opened wide,
as the church rapidly filled with the
fashionably dressed, perfumed, rustling,
and self-conscious throng.

Her heart beat quickly. The rebellious thoughts that will arise in the most
philosophical of us surged in her small
heavily gowned bosom. For her were
the gray things, the neutral tinted skies,
the ugly garb, the coarse meats; for
them the rainbow, the ethereal airiness
of earthly joys, the bonbons and glacés
of the world. Sister Josepha did not
know that the rainbow is elusive, and
its colours but the illumination of
tears; she had never been told that
earthly ethereality is necessarily ephem-
eral, nor that bonbons and glacés,
whether of the palate or of the soul,
nauseate and pall upon the taste. Dear
God, forgive her, for she bent with

contrite tears over her worn rosary, and glanced no more at the worldly glitter of femininity.

The sunbeams streamed through the high windows in purple and crimson lights upon a veritable fugue of colour. Within the seats, crush upon crush of spring millinery; within the aisles erect lines of gold-braided, gold-buttoned military. Upon the altar, broad sweeps of golden robes, great dashes of crimson skirts, mitres and gleaming crosses, the soft neutral hue of rich lace vestments; the tender heads of childhood in picturesque attire; the proud, golden magnificence of the domed altar with its weighting mass of lilies and wide-eyed roses, and the long candles that sparkled their yellow star points above the reverent throng within the altar rails.

The soft baritone of the Cardinal intoned a single phrase in the suspended

silence.   The censer took up the note in
its delicate clink clink, as it swung to and
fro in the hands of a fair-haired child.
Then the organ, pausing an instant in
a deep, mellow, long-drawn note, burst
suddenly into a magnificent strain, and
the choir sang forth, "Kyrie Eleïson,
Christe Eleïson." One voice, flute-like,
piercing, sweet, rang high over the rest.
Sister Josepha heard and trembled, as
she buried her face in her hands, and let
her tears fall, like other beads, through
her rosary.

It was when the final word of the
service had been intoned, the last peal
of the exit march had died away, that
she looked up meekly, to encounter a
pair of youthful brown eyes gazing
pityingly upon her.   That was all she
remembered for a moment, that the
eyes were youthful and handsome and
tender.   Later, she saw that they were
placed in a rather beautiful boyish face,

surmounted by waves of brown hair,
curling and soft, and that the head was
set on a pair of shoulders decked in
military uniform.   Then the brown
eyes marched away with the rest of the
rear guard, and the white-bonneted sisters filed out the side door, through
the narrow court, back into the brown
convent.

That night Sister Josepha tossed
more than usual on her hard bed,
and clasped her fingers often in prayer
to quell the wickedness in her heart.
Turn where she would, pray as she
might, there was ever a pair of tender,
pitying brown eyes, haunting her persis-
tently.   The squeaky organ at vespers
intoned the clank of military accoutre-
ments to her ears, the white bonnets of
the sisters about her faded into mists
of curling brown hair.   Briefly, Sister
Josepha was in love.

The days went on pretty much as

before, save for the one little heart that beat rebelliously now and then, though it tried so hard to be submissive. There was the morning work in the refectory, the stupid little girls to teach sewing, and the insatiable lamps that were so greedy for oil. And always the tender, boyish brown eyes, that looked so sorrowfully at the fragile, beautiful little sister, haunting, following, pleading.

Perchance, had Sister Josepha been in the world, the eyes would have been an incident. But in this home of self-repression and retrospection, it was a life-story. The eyes had gone their way, doubtless forgetting the little sister they pitied; but the little sister?

The days glided into weeks, the weeks into months. Thoughts of escape had come to Sister Josepha, to flee into the world, to merge in the great city where recognition was impossible, and, working her way like the rest of humanity, perchance encounter the eyes again.

It was all planned and ready. She would wait until some morning when the little band of black-robed sisters wended their way to mass at the Cathedral. When it was time to file out the side-door into the courtway, she would linger at prayers, then slip out another door, and unseen glide up Chartres Street to Canal, and once there, mingle in the throng that filled the wide thoroughfare. Beyond this first plan she could think no further. Penniless, garbed, and shaven though she would be, other difficulties never presented themselves to her. She would rely on the mercies of the world to help her escape from this torturing life of inertia. It seemed easy now that the first step of decision had been taken.

The Saturday night before the final day had come, and she lay feverishly nervous in her narrow little bed, wondering with wide-eyed fear at the morrow. Pale-eyed Sister Dominica and Sister Francesca were whispering together in the dark silence, and Sister Josepha's ears pricked up as she heard her name.

"She is not well, poor child," said Francesca. "I fear the life is too confining."

"It is best for her," was the reply. "You know, sister, how hard it would be for her in the world, with no name but Camille, no friends, and her beauty; and then —"

Sister Josepha heard no more, for her heart beating tumultously in her bosom drowned the rest. Like the rush of the bitter salt tide over a drowning man clinging to a spar, came the complete submerging of her hopes of another life. No name but Camille, that was true; no nationality, for she

could never tell from whom or whence
she came; no friends, and a beauty
that not even an ungainly bonnet and
shaven head could hide. In a flash she
realised the deception of the life she
would lead, and the cruel self-torture
of wonder at her own identity. Already,
as if in anticipation of the world's questionings, she was asking herself, " Who
am I? What am I ? "

The next morning the sisters du
Sacré Cœur filed into the Cathedral at
High Mass, and bent devout knees
at the general confession. " Confiteor
Deo omnipotenti," murmured the priest;
and tremblingly one little sister followed
the words, " Je confesse à Dieu, tout
puissant — que j'ai beaucoup péché par
pensées — c'est ma faute — c'est ma
faute — c'est ma très grande faute."

The organ pealed forth as mass
ended, the throng slowly filed out, and
the sisters paced through the courtway

back into the brown convent walls. One paused at the entrance, and gazed with swift longing eyes in the direction of narrow, squalid Chartres Street, then, with a gulping sob, followed the rest, and vanished behind the heavy door.

THE PRALINE WOMAN

THE PRALINE WOMAN

THE praline woman sits by the side of
the Archbishop's quaint little old chapel
on Royal Street, and slowly waves her
latanier fan over the pink and brown
wares.

" Pralines, pralines. Ah, ma'amzelle,
you buy ? S'il vous plaît, ma'amzelle,
ces pralines, dey be fine, ver' fresh.

" Mais non, maman, you are not
sure ?

" Sho', chile, ma bébé, ma petite, she
put dese up hissef. He's hans' so small,
ma'amzelle, lak you's, mais brune. She
put dese up dis morn'. You tak' none ?
No husban' fo' you den !

" Ah, ma petite, you tak' ? Cinq
sous, bébé, may le bon Dieu keep you
good !

" Mais oui, madame, I know you étrangér. You don' look lak dese New Orleans peop'. You lak' dose Yankee dat come down 'fo' de war."

Ding-dong, ding-dong, ding-dong, chimes the Cathedral bell across Jackson Square, and the praline woman crosses herself.

" Hail, Mary, full of grace —

" Pralines, madame? You buy lak' dat? Dix sous, madame, an' one lil' piece fo' lagniappe fo' madame's lil' bébé. Ah, c'est bon !

" Pralines, pralines, so fresh, so fine ! M'sieu would lak' some fo' he's lil' gal' at home? Mais non, what's dat you say ? She's daid ! Ah, m'sieu, 't is my lil' gal what died long year ago. Misère, misère !

" Here come dat lazy Indien squaw. What she good fo', anyhow? She jes' sit lak dat in de French Market an' sell her filé, an' sleep, sleep, sleep, lak' so in he's blanket. Hey, dere, you, Tonita, how goes you' beezness?

"Pralines, pralines! Holy Father, you give me dat blessin' sho'? Tak' one, I know you lak dat w'ite one. It tas' good, I know, bien.

"Pralines, madame? I lak' you' face. What fo' you wear black? You' lil' boy daid? You tak' one, jes' see how it tas'. I had one lil' boy once, he jes' grow 'twell he 's big lak' dis, den one day he tak' sick an' die. Oh, madame, it mos' brek my po' heart. I burn candle in St. Rocque, I say my beads, I sprinkle holy water roun' he's bed; he jes' lay so, he's eyes turn up, he say 'Maman, maman,' den he die! Madame, you tak' one. Non, non, no l'argent, you tak' one fo' my lil' boy's sake.

"Pralines, pralines, m'sieu? Who mak' dese? My lil' gal, Didele, of co'se. Non, non, I don't mak' no mo'.

Po' Tante Marie get too ol'.   Didele?
She's one lil' gal I 'dopt. I see her one
day in de strit.   He walk so; hit col'
she shiver, an' I say, 'Where you gone,
lil' gal ? ' and he can' tell. He jes' crip
close to me, an' cry so !   Den I tak'
her home wid me, and she say he's
name Didele.   You see dey wa'nt nobody dere. My lil' gal, she 's daid of de
yellow fever; my lil' boy, he 's daid, po'
Tante Marie all alone.   Didele, she
grow fine, she keep house an' mek'
pralines.   Den, when night come, she
sit wid he's guitar an' sing,

> " ' Tu l'aime ces trois jours,
>   Tu l'aime ces trois jours,
>   Ma cœur à toi,
>   Ma cœur à toi,
>   Tu l'aime ces trois jours ! '

" Ah, he's fine gal, is Didele !
" Pralines, pralines !   Dat lil' cloud,
h'it look lak' rain, I hope no.
" Here come dat lazy I'ishman down

de strit.   I don't lak' I'ishman, me,
non, dey so funny.   One day one
I'ishman, he say to me, 'Auntie, what
fo' you talk so?' and I jes' say back,
'What fo' you say " Faith an' be
jabers"?'   Non, I don' lak I'ishman,
me!

" Here come de rain !   Now I got
fo' to go.   Didele, she be wait fo' me.
Down h'it come !   H'it fall in de
Meesseesip, an' fill up — up — so,
clean to de levee, den we have big cri-
vasse, an' po' Tante Marie float away.
Bon jour, madame, you come again?
Pralines !   Pralines ! "

ODALIE

ODALIE

Now and then Carnival time comes at the time of the good Saint Valentine, and then sometimes it comes as late as the warm days in March, when spring is indeed upon us, and the greenness of the grass outvies the green in the royal standards.

Days and days before the Carnival proper, New Orleans begins to take on a festive appearance. Here and there the royal flags with their glowing greens and violets and yellows appear, and then, as if by magic, the streets and buildings flame and burst like poppies out of bud, into a glorious refulgence of colour that steeps the senses into a languorous acceptance of warmth and beauty.

On Mardi Gras day, as you know, it is a town gone mad with folly. A huge masked ball emptied into the streets at daylight; a meeting of all nations on common ground, a pot-pourri of every conceivable human ingredient, but faintly describes it all. There are music and flowers, cries and laughter and song and joyousness, and never an aching heart to show its sorrow or dim the happiness of the streets. A wondrous thing, this Carnival!

But the old cronies down in French-town, who know everything, and can recite you many a story, tell of one sad heart on Mardi Gras years ago. It was a woman's, of course; for "Il est toujours les femmes qui sont malheureuses," says an old proverb, and perhaps it is right. This woman — a child, she would be called elsewhere, save in this land of tropical growth and pre-cocity — lost her heart to one who

never knew, a very common story, by
the way, but one which would have
been quite distasteful to the haughty
judge, her father, had he known.

Odalie was beautiful. Odalie was
haughty too, but gracious enough to
those who pleased her dainty fancy.
In the old French house on Royal
Street, with its quaint windows and
Spanish courtyard green and cool,
and made musical by the plashing of
the fountain and the trill of caged birds,
lived Odalie in convent-like seclusion.
Monsieur le Juge was determined no
hawk should break through the cage
and steal his dove; and so, though there
was no mother, a stern duenna aunt
kept faithful watch.

Alas for the precautions of la Tante!
Bright eyes that search for other bright
eyes in which lurks the spirit of youth
and mischief are ever on the look-out,
even in church. Dutifully was Odalie

marched to the Cathedral every Sunday
to mass, and Tante Louise, nodding devoutly over her beads, could not see
the blushes and glances full of meaning,
a whole code of signals as it were, that
passed between Odalie and Pierre, the
impecunious young clerk in the court-
room.

Odalie loved, perhaps, because there
was not much else to do. When one
is shut up in a great French house with
a grim sleepy tante and no companions
of one's own age, life becomes a dull
thing, and one is ready for any new
sensation, particularly if in the veins
there bounds the tempestuous Spanish-
French blood that Monsieur le Juge
boasted of. So Odalie hugged the
image of her Pierre during the week
days, and played tremulous little love-
songs to it in the twilight when la Tante
dozed over her devotion book, and on
Sundays at mass there were glances

and blushes, and mayhap, at some especially remembered time, the touch of finger-tips at the holy-water font, while la Tante dropped her last genuflexion.

Then came the Carnival time, and one little heart beat faster, as the gray house on Royal Street hung out its many-hued flags, and draped its grim front with glowing colours. It was to be a time of joy and relaxation, when every one could go abroad, and in the crowds one could speak to whom one chose. Unconscious plans formulated, and the petite Odalie was quite happy as the time drew near.

"Only think, Tante Louise," she would cry, "what a happy time it is to be!"

But Tante Louise only grumbled, as was her wont.

It was Mardi Gras day at last, and early through her window Odalie could hear the jingle of folly bells on the maskers' costumes, the tinkle of music, and the echoing strains of songs. Up to her ears there floated the laughter of the older maskers, and the screams of the little children frightened at their own images under the mask and domino. What a hurry to be out and in the motley merry throng, to be pacing Royal Street to Canal Street, where was life and the world!

They were tired eyes with which Odalie looked at the gay pageant at last, tired with watching throng after throng of maskers, of the unmasked, of peering into the cartsful of singing minstrels, into carriages of revellers, hoping for a glimpse of Pierre the devout. The allegorical carts rumbling by with their important red-clothed horses were beginning to lose charm, the disguises showed tawdry, even the gay-hued flags fluttered sadly to Odalie.

Mardi Gras was a tiresome day, after all, she sighed, and Tante Louise agreed with her for once.

Six o'clock had come, the hour when all masks must be removed. The long red rays of the setting sun glinted athwart the many-hued costumes of the revellers trooping unmasked home-ward to rest for the night's last mad frolic.

Down Toulouse Street there came the merriest throng of all. Young men and women in dainty, fairy-like garb, dancers, and dresses of the pic-turesque Empire, a butterfly or two and a dame here and there with powdered hair and graces of olden time. Sing-ing with unmasked faces, they danced toward Tante Louise and Odalie. She stood with eyes lustrous and tear-heavy, for there in the front was Pierre, Pierre the faithless, his arms about the slen-der waist of a butterfly, whose tinselled

powdered hair floated across the lace
ruffles of his Empire coat.

"Pierre!" cried Odalie, softly. No
one heard, for it was a mere faint breath
and fell unheeded. Instead the laughing throng pelted her with flowers and
candy and went their way, and even
Pierre did not see.

You see, when one is shut up in the
grim walls of a Royal Street house, with
no one but a Tante Louise and a grim
judge, how is one to learn that in this
world there are faithless ones who may
glance tenderly into one's eyes at mass
and pass the holy water on caressing
fingers without being madly in love?
There was no one to tell Odalie, so she
sat at home in the dull first days of
Lent, and nursed her dear dead love,
and mourned as women have done from
time immemorial over the faithlessness
of man. And when one day she asked
that she might go back to the Ursulines'

convent where her childish days were
spent, only to go this time as a nun,
Monsieur le Juge and Tante Louise
thought it quite the proper and convenient thing to do; for how were
they to know the secret of that Mardi
Gras day?

LA JUANITA

LA JUANITA

IF you never lived in Mandeville, you cannot appreciate the thrill of wholesome, satisfied joy which sweeps over its inhabitants every evening at five o'clock. It is the hour for the arrival of the "New Camelia," the happening of the day. As early as four o'clock the trailing smoke across the horizon of the treacherous Lake Pontchartrain appears, and Mandeville knows then that the hour for its siesta has passed, and that it must array itself in its coolest and fluffiest garments, and go down to the pier to meet this sole connection between itself and the outside world; the little, puffy, side-wheel steamer that comes daily from New Orleans and brings the mail and the news.

On this particular day there was an air of suppressed excitement about the little knot of people which gathered on the pier. To be sure, there were no outward signs to show that anything unusual had occurred. The small folks danced with the same glee over the worn boards, and peered down with daring excitement into the perilous depths of the water below. The sun, fast sinking in a gorgeous glow behind the pines of the Tchefuncta region far away, danced his mischievous rays in much the same manner that he did every other day. But there was a something in the air, a something not tangible, but mysterious, subtle. You could catch an indescribable whiff of it in your inner senses, by the half-eager, furtive glances that the small crowd cast at La Juanita.

"Gar, gar, le bateau!" said one dark-tressed mother to the wide-eyed baby. "Et, oui," she added, in an undertone to her companion. "Voilà, La Juanita!"

La Juanita, you must know, was the pride of Mandeville, the adored, the admired of all, with her petite, half-Spanish, half-French beauty. Whether rocking in the shade of the Cherokee-rose-covered gallery of Grandpère Colomés' big house, her fair face bonnet-shaded, her dainty hands gloved to keep the sun from too close an acquaintance, or splashing the spray from the bow of her little pirogue, or fluffing her skirts about her tiny feet on the pier, she was the pet and ward of Mandeville, as it were, La Juanita Alvarez, since Madame Alvarez was a widow, and Grandpère Colomés was strict and stern.

And now La Juanita had set her small foot down with a passionate stamp before Grandpère Colomés' very face, and tossed her black curls about her wilful head, and said she would go to the pier this evening to meet her Mercer. All Mandeville knew this, and cast its furtive glances alternately at La Juanita with two big pink spots in her cheeks, and at the entrance to the pier, expecting Grandpère Colomés and a scene.

The sun cast red glows and violet shadows over the pier, and the pines murmured a soft little vesper hymn among themselves up on the beach, as the " New Camelia " swung herself in, crabby, sidewise, like a fat old gentleman going into a small door. There was the clang of an important bell, the scream of a hoarse little whistle, and Mandeville rushed to the gang-plank to welcome the outside world. Juanita put her hand through a waiting arm, and tripped away with her Mercer, big and blond and brawny. " Un Américain, pah ! " said the little mother

of the black eyes. And Mandeville
sighed sadly, and shook its head, and
was sorry for Grandpère Colomés.

This was Saturday, and the big regatta would be Monday. Ah, that
regatta, such a one as Mandeville had
never seen! There were to be boats
from Madisonville and Amite, from
Lewisburg and Covington, and even
far-away Nott's Point. There was to
be a Class A and Class B and Class C,
and the little French girls of the town
flaunted their ribbons down the one
oak-shaded, lake-kissed street, and dared
anyone to say theirs were not the
favourite colours.

In Class A was entered, "'La Juanita,' captain Mercer Grangeman, colours pink and gold." Her name, her
colours; what impudence!

Of course, not being a Mandevillian,
you could not understand the shame
of Grandpère Colomés at this. Was it

not bad enough for his petite Juanita,
his Spanish blossom, his hope of a family that had held itself proudly aloof from
" dose Americain " from time immemorial, to have smiled upon this Mercer,
this pale-eyed youth? Was it not bad
enough for her to demean herself by
walking upon the pier with him? But
for a boat, his boat, "un bateau Américain," to be named La Juanita! Oh,
the shame of it! Grandpère Colomés
prayed a devout prayer to the Virgin
that " La Juanita" should be capsized.

Monday came, clear and blue and
stifling. The waves of hot air danced
on the sands and adown the one street
merrily. Glassily calm lay the Pontchartrain, heavily still hung the atmosphere. Madame Alvarez cast an in-
quiring glance toward the sky. Grandpère Colomés chuckled. He had not
lived on the shores of the treacherous
Lake Pontchartrain for nothing. He

knew its every mood, its petulances and passions; he knew this glassy warmth and what it meant. Chuckling again and again, he stepped to the gallery and looked out over the lake, and at the pier, where lay the boats rocking and idly tugging at their moorings. La Juanita in her rose-scented room tied the pink ribbons on her dainty frock, and fastened cloth of gold roses at her lithe waist.

It was said that just before the crack of the pistol La Juanita's tiny hand lay in Mercer's, and that he bent his head, and whispered softly, so that the surrounding crowd could not hear, —

"Juanita mine, if I win, you will?"

"Oui, mon Mercere, eef you win."

In another instant the white wings were off scudding before the rising breeze, dipping their glossy boat-sides into the clear water, straining their cordage in their tense efforts to reach the stake boats. Mandeville indiscriminately distributed itself on piers, large and small, bath-house tops, trees, and craft of all kinds, from pirogue, dory, and pine-raft to pretentious cat-boat and shell-schooner. Mandeville cheered and strained its eyes after all the boats, but chiefly was its attention directed to " La Juanita."

" Ah, voilà, eet is ahead ! "

" Mais non, c'est un autre ! "

" La Juanita ! La Juanita ! "

" Regardez Grandpère Colomés ! "

Old Colomés on the big pier with Madame Alvarez and his granddaughter was intently straining his weather-beaten face in the direction of Nott's Point, his back resolutely turned upon the scudding white wings. A sudden chuckle of grim satisfaction caused La Petite's head to toss petulantly.

But only for a minute, for Grandpère Colomés' chuckle was followed by a shout of dismay from those whose glance had followed his. You must know that it is around Nott's Point that the storm king shows his wings first, for the little peninsula guards the entrance which leads into the southeast waters of the stormy Rigolets and the blustering Gulf. You would know, if you lived in Mandeville, that when the pines on Nott's Point darken and when the water shows white beyond like the teeth of a hungry wolf, it is time to steer your boat into the mouth of some one of the many calm bayous which flow silently throughout St. Tammany parish into the lake. Small wonder that the cry of dismay went up now, for Nott's Point was black, with a lurid light overhead, and the roar of the grim southeast wind came ominously over the water.

La Juanita clasped her hands and strained her eyes for her namesake.

The racers had rounded the second stake-boat, and the course of the triangle headed them directly for the lurid cloud.

You should have seen Grandpère Colomés then. He danced up and down the pier in a perfect frenzy. The thin pale lips of Madame Alvarez moved in a silent prayer; La Juanita stood coldly silent.

And now you could see that the advance guard of the southeast force had struck the little fleet. They dipped and scurried and rocked, and you could see the sails being reefed hurriedly, and almost hear the rigging creak and moan under the strain. Then the wind came up the lake, and struck the town with a tumultuous force. The waters rose and heaved in the long, sullen ground-swell, which betokened serious trouble. There was a rush of lake-craft to shelter. Heavy gray waves boomed against the

breakwaters and piers, dashing their
brackish spray upon the strained watch-
ers; then with a shriek and a howl the
storm burst full, with blinding sheets of
rain, and a great hurricane of Gulf wind
that threatened to blow the little town
away.

La Juanita was proud. When Grandpère and Madame led her away in the
storm, though her face was white, and
the rose mouth pressed close, not a
word did she say, and her eyes were as
bright as ever before. It was foolish
to hope that the frail boats could sur-
vive such a storm. There was not even
the merest excuse for shelter out in the
waters, and when Lake Pontchartrain
grows angry, it devours without pity.

Your tropical storm is soon over,
however, and in an hour the sun struggled through a gray and misty sky,
over which the wind was sweeping
great clouds. The rain-drops hung

diamond-like on the thick foliage, but the long ground-swell still boomed against the breakwaters and showed white teeth, far to the south.

As chickens creep from under shelter after a rain, so the people of Mandeville crept out again on the piers, on the bath-houses, on the breakwater edge, and watched eagerly for the boats. Slowly upon the horizon appeared white sails, and the little craft swung into sight. One, two, three, four, five, six, seven, eight, nine, counted Mandeville. Every one coming in! Bravo! And a great cheer that swept the whole length of the town from the post-office to Black Bayou went up. Bravo! Every boat was coming in. But — was every man?

This was a sobering thought, and in the hush which followed it you could hear the Q. and C. train thundering over the great lake-bridge, miles away.

Well, they came into the pier at last, "La Juanita" in the lead; and as Captain Mercer landed, he was surrounded by a voluble, chattering, anxious throng that loaded him with questions in patois, in broken English, and in French. He was no longer "un Américain" now, he was a hero.

When the other eight boats came in, and Mandeville saw that no one was lost, there was another ringing bravo, and more chattering of questions.

We heard the truth finally. When the storm burst, Captain Mercer suddenly promoted himself to an admiralship and assumed command of his little fleet. He had led them through the teeth of the gale to a small inlet on the coast between Bayou Lacombe and Nott's Point, and there they had waited until the storm passed. Loud were the praises of the other captains for Admiral Mercer, profuse were the thanks of the

sisters and sweethearts, as he was carried triumphantly on the shoulders of
the sailors adown the wharf to the
Maison Colomés.

The crispness had gone from Juanita's pink frock, and the cloth of gold
roses were wellnigh petalless, but the
hand that she slipped into his was
warm and soft, and the eyes that were
upturned to Mercer's blue ones were
shining with admiring tears. And even
Grandpère Colomés, as he brewed on
the Cherokee-rose-covered gallery, a
fiery punch for the heroes, was heard
to admit that "some time dose Americain can mos' be lak one Frenchman."

And we danced at the betrothal supper the next week.

TITEE

TITEE

It was cold that day. The great sharp north-wind swept out Elysian Fields Street in blasts that made men shiver, and bent everything in their track. The skies hung lowering and gloomy; the usually quiet street was more than deserted, it was dismal.

Titee leaned against one of the brown freight cars for protection against the shrill norther, and warmed his little chapped hands at a blaze of chips and dry grass. "Maybe it'll snow,'' he muttered, casting a glance at the sky that would have done credit to a practised seaman. "Then won't I have fun! Ugh, but the wind blows!"

It was Saturday, or Titee would have been in school, the big yellow school on Marigny Street, where he went every day when its bell boomed nine o'clock, went with a run and a joyous whoop, ostensibly to imbibe knowledge, really to make his teacher's life a burden.

Idle, lazy, dirty, troublesome boy, she called him to herself, as day by day wore on, and Titee improved not, but let his whole class pass him on its way to a higher grade. A practical joke he relished infinitely more than a practical problem, and a good game at pin-sticking was far more entertaining than a language lesson. Moreover, he was always hungry, and would eat in school before the half-past ten recess, thereby losing much good playtime for his voracious appetite.

But there was nothing in natural history that Titee did not know. He could dissect a butterfly or a mosquito hawk, and describe their parts as accurately as

a spectacled student with a scalpel and
microscope could talk about a cadaver.
The entire Third District, with its
swamps and canals and commons and
railroad sections, and its wondrous,
crooked, tortuous streets, was an open
book to Titee. There was not a nook
or corner that he did not know or
could not tell of. There was not a bit
of gossip among the gamins, little Creole and Spanish fellows, with dark skins
and lovely eyes, like spaniels, that
Titee could not tell of. He knew just
exactly when it was time for crawfish to
be plentiful down in the Claiborne and
Marigny canals; just when a poor,
breadless fellow might get a job in the
big bone-yard and fertilising factory,
out on the railroad track ; and as for
the levee, with its ships and schooners
and sailors, how he could revel in them !
The wondrous ships, the pretty little
schooners, where the foreign-looking

sailors lay on long moonlight nights, singing to their guitars and telling great stories, — all these things and more could Titee tell of. He had been down to the Gulf, and out on its treacherous waters through the Eads jetties on a fishing-smack with some jolly brown sailors, and could interest the whole school-room in the talk-lessons, if he chose.

Titee shivered as the wind swept round the freight-cars. There is n't much warmth in a bit of a jersey coat.

"Wish 'twas summer," he murmured, casting another sailor's glance at the sky. "Don't believe I like snow; it 's too wet and cold." And with a last parting caress at the little fire he had builded for a minute's warmth, he plunged his hands in his pockets, shut his teeth, and started manfully on his mission out the railroad track toward the swamps.

It was late when Titee came home, to such a home as it was, and he had but illy performed his errand; so his mother beat him and sent him to bed supperless. A sharp strap stings in cold weather, and a long walk in the teeth of a biting wind creates a keen appetite. But if Titee cried himself to sleep that night, he was up bright and early next morning, had been to mass, devoutly kneeling on the cold floor, blowing his fingers to keep them warm, and was home almost before the rest of the family were awake.

There was evidently some great matter of business on the young man's mind, for he scarcely ate his breakfast, and left the table soon, eagerly cramming the remainder of his meal in his pockets.

"Ma foi, but what now?" mused his mother, as she watched his little form sturdily trudging the track in the face of the wind; his head, with the rimless cap thrust close on the shock of black hair, bent low; his hands thrust deep in the bulging pockets.

"A new live play-toy h'it may be,' ventured the father; "he is one funny chil."

The next day Titee was late for school. It was something unusual, for he was always the first on hand to fix some plan of mechanism to make the teacher miserable. She looked reprovingly at him this morning, when he came in during arithmetic class, his hair all wind-blown, his cheeks rosy from a hard fight with the sharp blasts. But he made up for his tardiness by his extreme goodness all day; just think, Titee did not even eat once before noon, a something unparalleled in the entire previous history of his school life.

When the lunch-hour came, and all the yard was a scene of feast and fun,

one of the boys found him standing by
a post, disconsolately watching a ham
sandwich as it rapidly disappeared down
the throat of a sturdy, square-headed
little fellow.

"Hello, Edgar," he said, "what you
got fer lunch?"

"Nothin'," was the mournful reply.

"Ah, why don't you stop eatin' in
school, fer a change? You don't ever
have nothin' to eat."

"I did n't eat to-day," said Titee,
blazing up.

"You did!"

"I tell you I did n't!" and Titee's
hard little fist planted a punctuation
mark on his comrade's eye.

A fight in the schoolyard! Poor
Titee was in disgrace again. Still, in
spite of his battered appearance, a severe
scolding from the principal, lines to
write, and a further punishment from
his mother, Titee scarcely remained for

his dinner, but was off down the railroad track with his pockets partly
stuffed with the remnants of the scanty
meal.

And the next day Titee was tardy
again, and lunchless too, and the next,
until the teacher, in despair, sent a nicely
printed note to his mother about him,
which might have done some good, had
not Titee taken great pains to tear it up
on the way home.

One day it rained, whole bucketsful
of water, that poured in torrents from a
miserable, angry sky. Too wet a day
for bits of boys to be trudging to school,
so Titee's mother thought; so she kept
him at home to watch the weather
through the window, fretting and fuming like a regular storm in miniature. As
the day wore on, and the rain did not
abate, his mother kept a strong watch
upon him, for he tried many times to
slip away.

Dinner came and went, and the gray soddenness of the skies deepened into the blackness of coming night. Some-one called Titee to go to bed, and Titee was nowhere to be found.

Under the beds, in closets and cor-ners, in such impossible places as the soap-dish and water-pitcher even, they searched, but he had gone as completely as if he had been spirited away. It was of no use to call up the neighbors, he had never been near their houses, they affirmed, so there was nothing to do but to go to the railroad track where Titee had been seen so often trudging in the shrill north-wind.

With lanterns and sticks, and his little yellow dog, the rescuing party started down the track. The rain had ceased falling, but the wind blew a gale, scurrying great gray clouds over a fierce sky. It was not exactly dark, though in this part of the city there is neither gas nor electricity, and on such a night as this neither moon nor stars dared show their faces in so gray a sky; but a sort of all-diffused luminosity was in the air, as though the sea of atmosphere was charged with an ethereal phosphorescence.

Search as they did, there were no signs of Titee. The soft earth between the railroad ties crumbled between their feet without showing any small tracks or footprints.

"Mais, we may as well return," said the big brother; "he is not here."

"Oh, mon Dieu," urged the mother, "he is, he is; I know it."

So on they went, slipping on the wet earth, stumbling over the loose rocks, until a sudden wild yelp from Tiger brought them to a standstill. He had rushed ahead of them, and his voice could be heard in the distance, howling piteously.

With a fresh impetus the little muddy party hurried forward. Tiger's yelps could be heard plainer and plainer, mingled now with a muffled, plaintive little wail.

After a while they found a pitiful little heap of sodden rags, lying at the foot of a mound of earth and stones thrown upon the side of the track. It was Titee with a broken leg, all wet and miserable and moaning.

They picked him up tenderly, and started to carry him home. But he cried and clung to the mother, and begged not to go.

" Ah, mon pauvre enfant, he has the fever ! " wailed the mother.

" No, no, it 's my old man. He 's hungry," sobbed Titee, holding out a little package. It was the remnants of his dinner, all wet and rain-washed.

" What old man ? " asked the big brother.

"My old man. Oh, please, please don't go home till I see him. I'm not hurting much, I can go."

So, yielding to his whim, they carried him farther away, down the sides of the track up to an embankment or levee by the sides of the Marigny Canal. Then the big brother, suddenly stopping, exclaimed:

"Why, here's a cave. Is it Robinson Crusoe?"

"It's my old man's cave," cried Titee. "Oh, please go in; maybe he's dead."

There cannot be much ceremony in entering a cave. There is but one thing to do, — walk in. This they did, and holding up the lantern, beheld a weird sight. On a bed of straw and paper in one corner lay a withered, wizened, white-bearded old man with wide eyes staring at the unaccustomed light. In the other corner was an equally dilapidated cow.

"It's my old man!" cried Titee, joyfully. "Oh, please, grandpa, I couldn't get here to-day, it rained all mornin' an' when I ran away, I fell down an' broke something, an', oh, grandpa, I'm all tired an' hurty, an' I'm so 'fraid you're hungry."

So the secret of Titee's jaunts down the railroad was out. In one of his trips around the swamp-land, he had discovered the old man exhausted from cold and hunger in the fields. Together they had found this cave, and Titee had gathered the straw and paper that made the bed. Then a tramp cow, old and turned adrift, too, had crept in and shared the damp dwelling. And thither Titee had trudged twice a day, carrying his luncheon in the morning and his dinner in the afternoon.

"There's a crown in heaven for that child," said the officer of charity to whom the case was referred.

But as for Titee, when the leg was well, he went his way as before.